THE POLITICAL ACTION HANDBOOK:

A HOW TO GUIDE
FOR THE
HIP HOP GENERATION

Maya Rockeymoore, Ph.D.

www.MayaRockeymoore.com

Library of Congress Cataloging-in-Publication Data has been applied
for Rockeymoore, Maya, 1971-
    The political action handbook: a how to guide for the hip hop
    generation/
    Maya Rockeymoore.—1st ed.
    cm.
    Includes bibliographical references and index.

    ISBN 0-9759886-0-3 (paperback)

Cover Design by Debra Moore/Open Mind Design
Cover Photo (Nick White/Getty Images)
Author Photo (Point of View Studio)
Illustrations by Mark Rockeymoore

H^{2}G™

Printed in the United States of America.

For my father Thomas Charles "T.C." Rockeymoore, who continues to fly the U.S. flag in spite of all of the adversity and uncertainties he has faced in life.

CONTENTS

FOREWORD
By Michael Eric Dyson

As I spoke at the historic National Hip-Hop Political Convention in Newark this past June, I was struck by the great hunger of young black folk to translate their generation's artistic energy into substantive political action. The knock on the hip-hop generation – that they aren't involved in politics or "the movement" – is by now a lazy mantra repeated by elders who are turned off by the baggy clothes and boisterous chatter of the young. But what isn't often repeated, though it's nonetheless true, is that most folk in the civil rights generation weren't directly involved either. In fact, Martin Luther King, Jr. was pressed to explain in his famous 1965 *Playboy* magazine interview why more Negroes weren't flooding the streets and rallying to the cause of their own freedom. So if there's political lethargy and social apathy in this generation, it surely didn't start here, which is an important point to make if we're going to move beyond finger-pointing to problem-solving.

The truth is that hip-hop was born in political pain and social misery. By the time hip-hop surfaced as an intriguing form of cultural expression, Ronald Reagan had just risen to power. "Re-Ron," as hip-hop progenitor Gil Scott-Heron colorfully dubbed him, practiced presidential politics as a séance of sorts: he conjured the spirits of conservatives who had gone before him and added his ventriloquist's voice to their legacies by making already bleak urban landscapes even bleaker. The suffering of the poorest members of our society got worse: their schools were neglected (how else could it be when Reagan, in a move designed to defend malnourished lunch programs, declared ketchup a vegetable?); their neighborhoods faced shrunken resources; their jobs disappeared; and the underground economy flourished, especially in the Age of Crack.

Near its beginning, hip-hop found it's political voice in groups like Grandmaster Flash and the Furious Five. The quintet's 1982 anthem "The Message" drew a searing portrait of hustlers, pimps, pan-handlers, stressed parents, vulnerable children – and a blighted urban landscape that was so accurately and poignantly pitched that it actually seemed to speak and became the song's most memorable character. Its refrain was instantly unforgettable and came to symbolize the plight of the poor: "It's like a jungle sometimes/ It makes me wonder how I keep from going under."

The task of the hip-hop artist was to keep its followers from going under, at least without a fight or a witness. In its golden age aspirations, hip-hop sought to spit venom at the powers and people that kept their feet on the necks of the disadvantaged. At their best, hip-hop groups like Public Enemy encouraged their brothers and sisters – this was, after all, an era of rap that tried to draw its kinship from the blood of the ancestors, not to impose it's will through the blood on the streets – to "fight the powers that be." Still, gangsta rap with its hardcore sensibilities wasn't far behind, and at least initially, it gained its bona fides by proving how it could tether its politics to its pimp-walk and gangbanging.

Don't forget that it was former N.W.A. front man Ice Cube – more than a decade before he found cinematic riches in the barbershop, and immediately after he decamped from gangsta rap's most notorious group to become it's foremost poet before 2Pac – who presciently raised the question, "Why more niggas in the pen than in college?/ Now 'cause of that line I might be your cellmate/ That's from the nigga ya love to hate." It would take nearly fifteen years for a heralded 2003 report by the Justice Policy Institute, entitled "Cellblock or Classrooms? The Funding for Higher Education and Corrections and Its Impact on African American Men," to substantiate what Cube and millions of others understood: the nation spends much more money to incarcerate rather than educate young blacks.

If it appears ironic to some, even tragic to others that this wisdom spilled from the lips of a rapper, and not a civil rights leader, it's a measure of the times in which we live. As the heroic examples and historic struggles of the civil rights generation have been erased, distorted, or worshipped into irrelevance, the hip-hop generation has been largely deprived of a vital source of social imagination and political vision. We've got to get beyond members of the older generations haranguing youth for their materialism and their misbegotten social etiquette, and some young folk thinking that old heads are relics of a bygone era with little to offer them.

The older folk had an advantage that the youth don't possess: a social movement that sprang into action because the enemies were clear and the battles to be waged were obvious. Nowadays, things, and enemies, are much more fuzzy and ill-defined. Plans of action aren't always so easy to design or to follow. That doesn't mean that there's any less oppression than there was before; it simply means that the assault is coming from so many directions at the same time that we must be even more disciplined in our analysis and our clamor for response.

The harsh problems that our folk confront – diminished social opportunities, ephemeral employment at the periphery of the economy, the proliferation of incarceration, the re-segregation of public schools, the stigma of black youth, and the surrender of the genuine social will to improve the lot of the poorest – can only be answered by the sustained quest for workable remedies. Beyond its artistic creations in hip-hop culture – creations that have no doubt circulated globally and brought enhanced economic possibilities for many that would otherwise slip through the cracks of our culture and economy – this generation faces persistent social ills that must be matched by political prudence and engagement.

In short, we must figure out how to leverage the seismic presence in the cultural landscape of hip-hop into an equally powerful political juggernaut that testifies to the resilient will of its creators. Hip-hop pioneer Russell Simmons, with his Hip-Hop Summits, and hip-hop impresario Sean "P. Diddy" Combs, with his Citizen Change, seek to encourage black youth to organize their political power through activism and to channel their influence through the electoral process. But these admirable actions must be accompanied by intelligent reflection on the best means to achieve political maturity and power.

That's why Dr. Maya Michelle Rockeymoore's book, *The Political Action Handbook: A How-To Guide for the Hip Hop Generation*, is so important. She is one of the most talented and sophisticated political figures of the hip-hop generation. Armed with a Ph.D. and yet equipped with common sense, she has addressed political and public policy issues as diverse as Social Security, welfare reform, and the impact of climate change on black Americans. In this timely tome, Rockeymoore lays out specific details about how the political process can work for young black folk – and indeed, for *all* Americans. She tackles the importance of voting and clears away misconceptions about the voting process.

Rockeymoore also discusses the role of cash in politics, and shines a light on how fundraising and lobbying are critical to hip-hop political agency. She shows a flair for history and digs into the profound traditions and uses of protest that have sustained black social activism throughout our history. Rockeymoore discusses the need for younger candidates to run for office, and lucidly explains the advantages of volunteering on a political campaign and working in a political office. She skillfully lays bare the raison d'etre of networking and coalition-building and the boon of creating advocacy organizations to argue on behalf of often forgotten constituencies. Finally, Rockeymoore argues for using the incredible fertility and artistic creativity of hip-hop as "a platform for shaping public opinion and expanding political influence."

It should be obvious that one needn't be a member of the hip-hop generation to learn from Rockeymoore's wise and thoughtful book. Anyone who's interested in making the ideals and principles of democracy a living reality can benefit from using this handbook of political action. But for those members of the hip-hop generation who yearn to translate the huge commercial success and cultural visibility of an art form into flesh and blood politics, one couldn't ask for a better book than this one, or a more informed and passionate guide than Maya Rockeymoore.

ACKNOWLEDGEMENTS

Although I believe this book was divinely inspired, there are many earthly beings of heavenly descent that have guided me through the process of developing this manuscript. First and foremost has been my ever-faithful family whose loving support inspired me to continue plodding toward a path of completion. My parents Thomas and Hazel Rockeymoore, my sister Meredith Rockeymoore Brooks, and my brother Mark Rockeymoore, have been solid as a rock—reading versions of the manuscript and making wonderful suggestions along the way. Mark has even been so kind as to lend his numerous talents to this project in the form of the fantastic illustrations interspersed throughout the text. U.S. Rep. Elijah Cummings has also been a terrific supporter by helping me crystallize my thoughts, reading multiple drafts, providing guidance in those areas where he has infinite expertise, and referring my project to individuals whom he thought could be helpful.

A chain of serendipitous encounters has also shaped the creation of this book. It was in Brazil where I asked Dr. Julianne Malveaux advice on how to get the book published. She referred me to the talented team of professionals at Black Classic Press in Baltimore, Maryland. A chance discussion with Dr. Mischa Thompson led to a referral to my insightful editor, Ms. Dawn Marie Daniels. Another chance discussion with Clarence Brown introduced me to my talented cover artist Ms. Debra Moore of Open Mind Design. The hard-driving focus of Ms. Janice Lythcott Hill resulted in numerous referrals in the public relations and media fields. Others who have been essential to the development of this project include: U.S. Rep. William Jefferson, Weldon Rougeau, Marc Morial, Sen. Carl Andrews, Dr. Jewel Prestage, U.S. Rep. Charles Rangel, U.S. Rep. Melvin Watt, Ms. Sandy Wise, Dr. Phoebe Farris, Dr. Mack Jones, Ms. Tracey Walker, Ms. Jennifer Cummings, and Mr. Troy Clair.

PREQUEL

The idea to write this guidebook came to me as I was sitting in on a Hip Hop & Politics panel during Reverend Jesse Jackson's Wall Street Project in January of 2003. As the panelists gave their perspectives on the importance of younger African Americans becoming politically active, one young man about 18 years of age stood and asked about specific things that he could do to become more politically involved. A few of the panelists spoke abstractly about personal empowerment and the importance of registering to vote. But the young man, apparently feeling dissatisfied with these answers, then asked where he could get more information about how to become more politically active. None of the panelists had an immediate answer. One panelist replied vaguely that there were Web sites "out there." Finally, Davey D, a prominent West Coast DJ and Hip Hop activist, said that he would take the email addresses of the audience members and get back to them with some helpful resources.

It was at that moment that it occurred to me that the Hip Hop Generation could use a guidebook that not only contained a one-stop-shopping guide to websites, publications, organizations and other useful political resources, but that also provided basic, easy to follow steps for exerting power within the United States political context. Born in the post-Civil Rights era, I am one of many young Americans who grew up surrounded by the lyrics and style of the Hip Hop genre. Most in my generation never had direct experience with de jure segregation, yet we continue to live in a world of racially nuanced code words and staggering racial and class disparities in areas like health, education, and criminal justice. While many of my generation correctly interpret these outcomes as lasting forms of discrimination, the fact remains that a significant number have not made the connection on how to leverage their political power to build upon the legacy of the Civil Rights Movement and create positive change.

In my case, an early political education fostered by my parents led to activism in my youth and a desire to learn as much as possible about the political system that governs our lives. My quest informed my decision to study political science. It also led me to volunteer on my first campaign at the age of 19, become an activist in protest marches and demonstration rallies in my early twenties, organize and participate in fundraising events, and embark upon a career in the political arena that has included work on the powerful House Ways and Means Committee, in the offices of prominent members of Congress such as Reps. Melvin Watt and Charles Rangel, and in a Washington, D.C. policy think tank. Every one of these experiences occurred before I reached the age of 30.

By writing this book, it is my goal to share the knowledge that I have gained through my education, work and personal experiences to empower others to become more familiar with and active in the political process.

This book project has a tone of urgency because of the tremendous gravity of what is at stake if the Hip Hop Generation fails to become educated about what is happening to them, why it is happening, and what they can do to confront the people, systems, and policies that would cripple them before they've had a chance to enter the race.

In an age where civics and government courses have often been the first casualty in cash-strapped public schools seeking to balance scarce resources with the vast educational needs of students, this book serves as one small way to help close the critical gap in civics education. It is my hope that many who read this book find the information useful and, better still, use it as the basis for personal political action.

Intro: H²G—The Vital Element

This empowerment guide is about "The Man," "The System" and how the Hip Hop Generation can influence "The Game" ruling both. For 228 years, the U.S. has promoted an image of itself as a shining example of a democracy that honors individual rights and civic participation while living up to the ideals of truth, justice and freedom. The reality is much different from the hype. The U.S. has a constitutional republic form of government that has embraced numerous laws and practices that have, at one time or another, systematically denied most of its residents--poor whites, African Americans, Hispanics, women—their right to exercise their full democratic privileges as United States citizens.

What most of us do not learn in school is that even though the U.S. declared its independence from Britain in 1776, it took a full 189 years— with the passage of the Voting Rights Act of 1965—for the country to become truly democratic by allowing all citizens to freely participate in the electoral process under the protection of federal law. And, the only reason the U.S. reached a point of full enfranchisement is because of the efforts and sacrifice of each of the groups previously excluded. They challenged "The System"—the institutions of government and business—and "The Man"—the privileged few who pull the strings—to gain access to "The Game"—forms of civic participation that give groups power in government decisions that affect our lives.

Today, despite having no formal barriers to political participation, there are some who do not participate in the political process. Some, mostly younger people, say that they choose to remain disengaged because they are not interested, believe their voices are not heard, or prefer to exercise their right to self-determination using other

1

strategies. Vast numbers of these people—members of the Hip Hop Generation (or H^{2}G), remain disengaged because they do not know how to play The Game or fully realize why it is important to do so.

A Hip Hop Call to Action

Perhaps one of the most powerful cohorts of all time, the Hip Hop Generation is loosely defined as those 40 years of age and younger who grew to maturity surrounded by the style, vision, and sound of Hip Hop music and culture.[1] Our generation is powerful because it has used unprecedented creativity, resourcefulness, and brainpower to become a cultural and marketing phenomenon recognized around the globe. From London to Tokyo, Nairobi to Rio, Hip Hop music is embraced by those attracted to its irresistible beats, edgy lyrics and irreverent style.

Aside from its global platform, there are many additional strengths of our generation that often go unrecognized. Coalition building is one key aspect of Hip Hop that makes it a potential force to be reckoned with. The culture of Hip Hop bonds young people together across race, ethnicity, gender, class, religion, and nationality. While individuals may have different perspectives on narrow issues or even disagreements about elements of the genre, their lifestyles, preferences, and habits are greatly influenced by the common denominator of Hip Hop.

Another unrecognized, but potential strength of the Hip Hop Generation lies in its ability to embrace and dominate capital markets. From t-shirts and jeans to tennis shoes and jewelry, the buying power of the H^{2}G fuels the economic growth of entire industries and provides a vital base of financial support to local retail markets. While some may view this mostly uncritical embrace of capitalism and materialism as a weakness, the fact remains that Hip Hop artists, their music and videos set trends that drive consumers to select markets—generating billions of dollars in sales worldwide. Their collective market share presents a powerful economic base of influence that, if viewed from a strategic perspective and harnessed in creative and useful ways, can move mountains.

Of all the strengths belonging to the Hip Hop Generation, perhaps one of the most important lies in its power of analysis. The critical insight of master lyricists such as Grandmaster Flash and the Furious Five, KRS One and Boogie Down Productions, Chuck D and Public Enemy, Ice Cube, Ice T, Queen Latifah, Tupac, the Getto Boys, Goodie Mob, Lauryn Hill, Dead Prez, Nas, Mos Def, and Talib Kweli have been infused with distinctly political themes that articulate the people's desire for economic empowerment, freedom and justice. From education, drugs, violence, and housing to jobs, hunger, poverty, and health care, street scholars turned Hip Hop artists have accurately diagnosed the social ills impacting urban communities. What's more is that all of them have understood that these problems have been un-addressed or ineffectively addressed by The System.

As the lyrics suggest, there are a number of issues faced by the Hip Hop Generation that present obstacles to their quality of life and potential for future success. The grossly disproportionate percentage of African American men in prisons, the random and not-so-random violence perpetrated in urban communities, the skyrocketing rates of HIV/AIDS infection and other preventable chronic health conditions, the dysfunctional nature of the public (mis) education system, and the dramatic inequities in unemployment rates—especially among African-American teens and young adults—are a few of the depressing realities urban youth face daily. In the face of persistent inequities, the H^{2}G logically concludes that The System does not care about them or the challenges they face.

In addition to neglected social ills, the Hip Hop Generation is alienated further due to a perceived lack of established channels through which we can develop and engage new policy ideas or express opinions about social and political circumstances. While some have used the tools of popular culture (e.g. hip hop/rap, poetry, etc.) to express discontent with their plight and a few have actually found ways to directly engage the political system (e.g. campaign volunteers, congressional staff, interns, community organizations, etc.), countless others have been left without viable outlets through which they can articulate concerns and work constructively towards implementing solutions to the problems they see. Exacerbating this situation is the

3

perception that there is a lack of political will from policymakers to promote policy alternatives that would truly solve the problems.

What the H^2G must realize is that politicians, and The System in which they operate, are trained to respond to an organized, voting constituency. Politicians make calculated decisions about where to dedicate limited resources based on whom they believe is paying attention to their actions and whom they feel they are answerable to. As a result, individuals or groups that make their presence and preferences known through the ballot and by other means are more likely to receive attention and resources than those who do not. So, regardless of the connections Hip Hop may bring young people in the cultural and economic spheres, the fact remains that the H^2G is overlooked and disrespected in the political process because we are viewed as a disorganized, apathetic and disengaged mass.

Percent of 18-24 Year Olds That Voted in the 2000 Elections

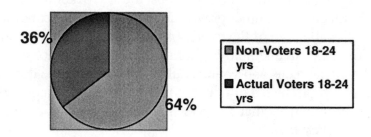

U.S. Census Bureau, 2002.

Nowhere is the unrealized potential of the Hip Hop Generation more evident than in its voting statistics. According to the U.S. Census Bureau, eligible voters under the age of 24 represent a block of 27 million votes yet only 36 percent of eligible voters 18-24 years of age voted in 2000.[2] Indeed, it is estimated that 39 million citizens aged 34 years and younger failed to vote in the 2000 presidential election.[3] Overall, Americans age 40 and younger represent a growing majority of the voting age population yet, if current trends continue,

4

the number of people 65 and older who vote in midterm elections is likely to exceed that of young people by a 4 to 1 ratio by 2022.[4] This phenomenon will ensure that public policies will continue to focus on issues that primarily benefit older populations.

The irony of it all is that the political power of the Hip Hop Generation is a sleeping giant that—if awakened—can (literally) rule the world. If one considers the narrow margin by which President George W. Bush managed to carry the elections in 2000, it is clear that a two to three percentage point increase in the number of young voters could have swung the elections in a different direction. This outcome would likely have resulted in vastly different policy decisions in both the domestic and international spheres. This example is only a modest glimpse at the potential power of the Hip Hop Generation. If the H^2G combined its potential electoral power with a comprehensive empowerment strategy, we could truly realize the power, glory, and wealth often portrayed in Hip Hop music videos.

What will it take to move the H^2G into a position of fully realized power? The answer lies in three interconnected parts: education, organization, and action. It is a fundamental premise of this book that—as a result of poor educational preparation in schools and at home—many in the Hip Hop Generation have not received an adequate civic education that empowers them to understand how they can use their talent, influence and wit to challenge The Man, The System, and The Game in a way that maximizes their control over their individual and collective destiny.

Under-funding and neglect in U.S. public schools have led to a dangerously weakened government affairs curriculum that fails to teach students how The System works. Strapped budgets have produced high school government teachers who lack expertise in the area, outdated text books that keep children ignorant of contemporary political history and misinformed about not-so-ancient U.S. history, and schools that lack the means to organize field trips to places, such as State Capitols and local council chambers, where students can see government at work. Indeed, there are young people graduating from Washington, D.C. high schools who have never entered the nation's Capitol—only two miles from where they have grown up.

Lack of teaching in the home environment is another reason for the gap in civics education that exists today. Many in the Hip Hop Generation have not seen their parents vote, have not heard people close to them discussing current political events, and have not been the beneficiaries of stories and discussions that place U.S. history in its proper context. For example, I am shocked by the number of people of the H^2G I meet who express that their parents and relatives never talked about what it was like living in a racially segregated society, never taught them about the fundamentals of the Civil Rights or women's rights struggles, or discussed the history of slavery, classism and sexism in America. Given this reality, this book contends that the first step in mobilizing the H^2G requires a return to the basics: government 101 so to speak. Indeed, this book is designed to help fill this educational gap.

Organization is the next step the H^2G will have to pursue in their quest for social and political empowerment. There are several layers of organization that will be necessary to fully leverage political power. The first is forming or joining one or several formal membership groups or associations with local chapters that can represent the Hip Hop Generation and serve as a vehicle for advancing their political and policy interests. Citizen Change run by Sean "P. Diddy" Combs, the Hip Hop Summit Action Network run by Benjamin Chavis Muhammed and Russell Simmons, the college chapters run by the National Association for the Advancement of Colored People, and the National Urban League Young Professionals organization all have the potential to evolve into such an entity. The second is creating a mobilization machine that can register the H^2G to vote, get them to the polls in large numbers, and spur them to participate in community meetings, protest activities and fundraisers when necessary. It is likely that the groups or associations, with heavy participation from their local chapters, can serve this mobilization role along with a media campaign to reinforce the voting message. The third layer of organization lies in developing a policy agenda that enumerates the issues or problems to be addressed as well as the preferred solutions to those problems. The final layer is developing a political strategy to advance the policy agenda. In order to affect change in line with the

6

policy agenda it has developed, the H^2G must have a political strategy that encompasses the local, state and federal levels of government.

The third and final step in the political empowerment equation is action. Once the four organizational layers are in place, it is imperative that the Hip Hop Generation fully participate in The System by enacting all elements of The Game—the various political activities (e.g. voting, fundraising, protesting, etc.) outlined in the following pages.

In sum, it is time to bring the full power of the Hip Hop Generation to bear on the U.S. political system. If the H^2G just sit on the sidelines with undirected complaints, we perpetuate the very system that we criticize and change nothing in the process. The Hip Hop Generation must move beyond its posture of critical inaction toward strategic civic activities that will allow us to claim control over our lives, our communities and our country.

Back to the Basics

In talking with my peers in the Hip Hop Generation, I have learned that most of us do not fully understand how the political process works. A common view portrays a process filled with fast-talking, dishonest politicians who engage in mysterious, unsavory and possibly illegal activities. Indeed, not only do most seem to be unclear about what elected officials do, they are also not fully aware of how political decisions affect their lives.

Branches of Government

While some politicians may be fast-talking and even dishonest, these stereotypes do not discount the real purpose that elected officials serve in the political process. Politicians are individuals elected by the voting public to federal, state, or local political offices. It is their job to make sure that the interests of the people who elect them are properly represented in the political and policymaking process. Depending on their branch of service—Executive (The President), Legislative (Congress), or Judicial (the Courts)—politicians are variously called elected officials, administration officials, policymakers, lawmakers, or legislators (many judges—while not considered politicians—are also elected by voters or appointed by politicians).

In theory, elected officials in the Legislative Branch are supposed to execute their job functions in four key ways: 1) listening to what their constituents (the voting and non-voting public) want and need by reading their letters, attending community events, office meetings, etc.; 2) developing laws or policy proposals that benefit their constituents; 3) voting for proposals that serve the best interests of their constituents; and, 4) explaining to their constituents how their decisions affect their families, communities and country. It is important to note that constituents aren't just individuals, they are also the businesses, organizations, and institutions located within (and sometimes outside of) the policymaker's geographical district. In addition to the basic functions outlined above, there are a host of other factors—such as money, influence and access–that also dictate how policymakers conduct themselves in office. These factors will also be discussed in the following pages.

Elected officials can help determine the economic, educational and social wellbeing of entire communities. Two very important tasks of elected officials in the Legislative Branch include making laws and allocating money. Elected officials are the gatekeepers for trillions of dollars in tax revenue—that is, money paid by anyone in the public old enough to purchase taxable merchandise, own property, or earn a paycheck. And, through budget processes taking place at the local, state and federal levels, they control which individuals, groups, communities, businesses, institutions, and countries receive U.S. taxpayer dollars, how much they receive, and the purpose for which they can use the money.

Elected officials in the Administrative Branch are responsible for administering the laws passed by the Legislative Branch. And, these elected officials and the bureaucrats they control also have quite a bit of authority through their ability to interpret how the laws should be implemented in society.

Officials in the Judicial Branch decide on how the law should be interpreted when there are differences in opinions and determine whether laws violate the U.S. Constitution.

Terms of Service

Elected officials are public servants who serve at the pleasure of ordinary citizens—like you and me. Every two, four, or six years (depending on the office) voters go to the polls to decide whether their elected officials deserve another term in office. Ultimately, these elected officials are judged by the quality of their leadership. Are they accessible to the public? Do they bring money or other resources back to their community or District? Do their decisions or voting record reflect the priorities of the people whom they serve? These are just a few questions that voters consider when deciding whether to allow elected officials to remain in office.

How a Bill Becomes a Law

So how do policy ideas become laws? Many in the Hip Hop Generation may remember the School House Rock cartoon that ran on Saturday mornings instructing kids across America about how a bill becomes a law. The federal legislative process remains generally the same: 1) a policy idea is introduced separately in the House and Senate of the U.S. Congress as a piece of legislation or a bill; 2) the merits of the bill are considered by the committee with authority, or jurisdiction, over the issue; 3) if it has merit, the bill is passed with or without changes by the committee and introduced to the full legislative body for its voting consideration; 4) if approved by a vote of the full body, the bill is referred to a conference session where versions of the bill are considered by each legislative chamber (i.e. House and Senate); 5) once the differences are reconciled in conference, the bill goes to the President for final consideration; and, 6) if approved, the President signs the bill into law. While variations of this process are practiced in local and state legislative bodies across the country, the point remains that from birth to death elected officials and the political process they preside over largely determine the multitude of laws that govern our lives.

The Importance of Politics and Policy

So what's the difference between politics and policy? In short, politics is the process of making law while policy is the product or outcome of that process. Politics can be considered The Game through which people and groups push their objectives in the interest of turning their ideals, needs and desires into the law of the land by which everyone must abide. To paraphrase Harold Lasswell, a famous political scientist, "politics is the process of determining who gets what, when and how." In this formulation, policy becomes the "who," "what," "when," and "how"—in effect, the substance of which laws are made. Through a pattern of incentives and disincentives, policies—loosely defined as a set of rules, laws, principles, benefits, penalties, prohibitions, entitlements, or resource allocations—and the politics that determine them can influence our personal behaviors, shape our families' financial circumstances and educational opportunities, and structure how we relate to each other in society.

The interests and biases of the people and groups who participate in the process heavily influence politics and policies. This results in unequal outcomes for segments of the population who either choose not to participate in the process, have ineffective strategies for participating, and/or have not built the internal capacity to engage the system due to lack of education, historical exclusion and discrimination, or a combination of both. Thus, some often cite the unfairness of policies that seemed heavily biased against or in favor of certain communities. For example, the disparities in crack and cocaine sentencing have caused many experts to point to the unfairness of establishing unequal sentences for different versions of the same substance. They say that class and racial discrimination play a role because the laws establish harsher penalties for poor, mostly minority crack users as compared to the lighter penalties for richer, mostly white cocaine users.

Because policies are not race, class, or gender neutral, it is imperative that groups representative of all demographics and interests in society mobilize to bring balance and equity to a system that is fundamentally designed to meet only the needs of those who effectively participate. It is especially important that we increase the number of the H^2G who are involved in the policymaking process so that we can influence the design of policies in such a way as to reduce

10

or eliminate the discriminatory impact of many laws that have been passed at the federal, state, and local levels.

For those who would claim that neither politics nor policy is of interest to them or their neighborhoods: think again. The political process and the policies they produce have everything to do with you. Politics and policy affects your life in many ways that include:

- Directing money to neighborhoods to build or improve roads, schools, apartments and houses
- Influencing the behavior of the police
- Reducing or increasing the amount of taxes you pay and thereby reducing or increasing the amount of money you have in your pocket
- Determining the amount of college tuition you pay
- Putting you (your momma and your Uncle Ray-Ray) in jail, determining how long they stay, and whether they will be put to death
- Denying you the right to vote because of a felony conviction
- Imposing a Draft that can force you to join the military and kill people in the name of the U.S. Government
- Influencing the type of health care that you receive or whether you receive health care at all
- Deciding at what age you are eligible to drive, how fast you can drive, and under what circumstances your driver's license can be suspended or revoked
- Determining who's eligible to own a gun
- Creating and financing helpful programs like job training, Head Start, Food Stamps, TANF, WIC and SSI.

As the examples above suggest, the policies generated from the political process shape almost every aspect of our lives. Yet, too often we are willing to take a back seat in the political decisions that result in the policies that most profoundly affect our lives. We know that policies as diverse as mandatory minimum sentencing, felon disenfranchisement laws, employer-based health insurance, school voucher programs, high stakes testing, and Section 8 housing certificates have distinct and mostly negative effects on underserved communities. Yet, because each of these politically driven policies represent significant and life-altering effects on our communities, it should be increasingly evident why it is important to have a say in how these decisions are made.

The following pages will provide more information about how the H^2G can have more say in important political and policy decisions. At this point, however, it is imperative to articulate the fundamental element that will be required in order to become empowered. What many do not realize is that neither politicians nor the policies they create are fixed. Public policies can be changed just as easily as politicians themselves can be voted out of office. You may ask how is it that politicians and the policies they create can be so vulnerable to change? The answer lays in the power of you—the vital element—an individual who is active and engaged in the political process through a combination of strategic and highly political activities.

The Master Plan

The goal of this book is to politically empower the Hip Hop Generation—although other segments of the population may also find it useful—by identifying ten simple ways in which the H^2G of all backgrounds can influence the political process. This book seeks to provide practical steps for empowerment while illustrating how various and often untapped forms of political activity can make a difference.

Verse One discusses the importance of voting and common misperceptions about the voting process. Every two, four or six years registered voters receive an opportunity to elect or eject the politicians that represent them at the local, state and federal levels. While it is not the intent of this book to promote voting as the end all and be all of political participation, it is certainly an important and essential first step in asserting your political preferences and having control over how your life is governed.

While the vote is a necessary and important form of political expression, there are a host of other—equally legitimate—tools that people can use to influence the political process. Verse Two talks about the very important, but almost completely ignored role of fundraising. Fat cat corporate lobbyists have long known that money can actually be used to influence the political process, yet most— particularly African Americans and other minorities—have not utilized this political tool to its full potential. To be fair, most of us do not have much money to spare and what little we can contribute we believe is unlikely to make a difference. This Verse discusses these issues and ways that the Hip Hop Generation can overcome them to use fundraising to its advantage.

Protest is a tried and true form of political participation that has been used by millions over the years. From ancient civilizations to modern societies, protest has been used to challenge unpopular political regimes, confront societal injustices, advocate for goods and services that improve the quality of lives, and promote other forms of social change. Verse Three discusses the value of protest, the types of protest actions commonly used, and practical considerations for would-be protestors.

From welfare moms to food stamp recipients and Medicaid beneficiaries, poor people and people of color have been traditionally seen as receiving more government assistance than any other segment of U.S. society. Despite this stereotype, what most do not know is that corporations, associations, and other groups like farmers have their "hand out" receiving regular government assistance at levels far beyond those received by historically underserved populations. These entities are most often represented by professional lobbyists who lurk the halls of Congress seeking legislative fixes on behalf of their clients. Verse Four examines the lobbying process and discusses why the Hip Hop Generation needs to add lobbying to its portfolio of political empowerment tools.

The Rev. Al Sharpton, the late Sonny Bono, Arianna Huffington, Nelson Mandela, Shirley Chisholm, Arnold Schwarzenegger, and Rev. Jesse Jackson all have something in common: each of them has run for political office. Verse Five examines this form of political participation, discusses the importance of younger candidates tossing their hats into the ring, and provides practical guidelines for those who may want to pursue this option. If running for office is too serious a commitment for you, then volunteering on a political campaign—the

13

focus of Verse Six—or working in a political office—Verse Seven's topic—can give you the exposure and experience you need to gain more insight and influence into the political process.

Most do not think of networking as a strategy for political empowerment, yet it remains one of the most important and effective tools that we can utilize to strengthen our communities. The importance and potential of networking or coalition-building, therefore, is the focus of Verse Eight. If you are the type of person who likes to effect change from the outside and working for a government official doesn't appeal to you, then joining, working for, or creating an advocacy organization, the subjects of Verse Nine, may present the best alternatives for you. Finally, the Hip Hop Generation is most noted for its amazing creativity, dazzling talent and seemingly unlimited resourcefulness. The H^2G has had greater access to mass media outlets than previous generations and this has facilitated opportunities to amplify our creative products to a global audience. Verse Ten examines the relevance of using artistic expression such as lyrics, music, poetry, or prose as a platform for shaping public opinion and expanding political influence.

Various lessons from U.S. history have taught us that we cannot leave American-style democracy on autopilot when it comes to righting wrongs or strengthening our communities. In order to achieve a truly free and democratic society, Americans of all ages must maintain continuous and proactive engagement in the political and policy decisions of our country. The Hip Hop Generation in particular must get away from standing on the sidelines of life complaining about poor conditions or inadequate policies without doing what it takes to influence these decisions.

Even though many young people have bought into the hype that they aren't politically involved or interested, this conclusion ignores a stark reality: young people have been at the forefront of almost every contemporary social movement that has influenced the political process and made a difference in the quality of life for people in the U.S. and around the world. From the Civil Rights Movement, Women's Rights Movement and Vietnam to the anti-apartheid movement in South Africa, the fight for democracy in China, and new

14

anti-war and anti-globalization efforts, students and other young people have dedicated their time, energy and passion to achieving political change.

In light of this reality, this book argues that the Hip Hop Generation must dismiss self-defeating attitudes and misleading claims about youthful indifference in order to carry on the tradition of taking positive steps to make the world a better place. Clearly, young people have demonstrated that they can exert power strong enough to change the way political systems operate at local, state and federal levels. It is time to shatter the myth of disinterest that too often becomes a self-fulfilling prophecy of inaction and alienation. The Hip Hop Generation must realize its power and harness it in ways that increase their influence on the policy decisions that govern our lives. Let the games and gains begin.

(Re)SOURCES
Internet

Ben's Guide to U.S. Government   http://bensguide.gpo.gov
(Explore this unique, age-appropriate interactive tutorial and learn more about the branches of government, how laws are made, and the election process)

FirstGov.gov   www.firstgov.gov
(Get a detailed listing of all of the branches and levels of U.S. government and find the homepage for your state)

The National Archives Experience
www.archives.gov/national_archives_experience/charters/charters.html
(View a state-of-the-art online learning tutorial outlining The Declaration of Independence, The Constitution, and The Bill of Rights)

The Library of Congress   www.loc.gov
(View information about Congressional votes and legislation on THOMAS and other historical information)

Books

Sobel, Syl and Pam Tanzey. How The U.S. Government Works.
 Barron's Educational Series. 1999.

"Y'all tellin me that I need to get out and vote, huh. Why?
Ain't nobody black runnin but crackers, so, why I got to register?
I'm thinking of better shit to do with my time."
Outkast, "Git Up, Git Out." <u>Southernplayalisticadillacmuzik</u>. LaFace (1994)

Verse 1: Get Your Vote On!

On November 5, 2003 Waller County District Attorney Oliver
Kitzman published an open letter in the *Waller Times* stating that
college students at nearby Prairie View A&M University—a
historically black university located on the site of a former plantation
in Texas—would be subject to a $10,000 fine and a possible 10 years
in prison should they attempt to vote in local elections. Arguing that
students' votes were illegal because they were not permanent residents
of the county, Kitzman—who is white—feared that PV student votes
would dilute the value of the county's "real" residents. And fear he
should, with Prairie View students making up about 4,000 registered
voters in a county of only 27,000 and an estimated 20 percent of the
voting population, the actual and potential voting strength of Prairie
View students could determine the outcome of local elections.[5] In the
words of Texas State Senator Rodney Ellis, Prairie View students
could use their electoral power to literally control the entire Waller
County political and economic infrastructure if they so desired.

In the face of the D.A.'s voter suppression and intimidation tactics,
Prairie View students bravely challenged the Waller County power
structure to protect their right to vote. In January of 2004, the students
staged a 5,000 person strong march to the Waller County Courthouse
to protest the violation of their civil rights and turned out in full force
to attend a town hall meeting co-sponsored by the Congressional Black
Caucus and Rap the Vote. With the help of the NAACP Legal
Defense Fund, American Civil Liberties Union, and People for the
American Way, the students filed two lawsuits: one against Oliver
Kitzman and another seeking extended hour early voting days on the
college campus. At the request of Rep. Elijah Cummings, Chairman
of the Congressional Black Caucus and Rep. Sheila Jackson Lee, the
U.S. Department of Justice also launched an investigation to determine
whether a violation of the students' civil rights had indeed occurred.

Ironically, this was not the first brush with the law that Prairie View students had undergone with respect to their right to vote. In 1979, a court case brought by the students went all the way to the U.S. Supreme Court after several were indicted for voting in the Waller County general elections. This case, Symms vs. U.S., resulted in a landmark decision that upheld the right of college students to vote where they attend school even if they don't know whether they will live there permanently. Similarly, in 1992, nine students were arrested and booked in the county jail after voting in the Waller County elections. County officials claimed that the students voted fraudulently as their voter registration information could not be verified. Officials backed off only after the students, once again, organized a protest march to the county courthouse to protest the students' treatment.

Prairie View's story is important because it underscores the fact that at the dawn of the twenty-first century and 39 years after passage of the Voting Rights Act of 1965, the U.S. faces remnants of the same tactics of exclusion and fraud that characterized its sham of a democracy in the first 188 years of its existence. Even worse, Prairie View's story is not an isolated incident, but reflects a discernable pattern of voter intimidation most grossly symbolized by the shady chain of events that took place in Florida during the 2000 presidential elections. Following talk of ballot fraud and stolen elections in 2000, legislators at the federal, state, and local levels turned to paperless, electronic ballot machines in an attempt to secure the integrity of the voting process. However, experts claim that—without a paper receipt to verify ballots cast—even this measure is subject to widespread manipulation, fraud and abuse. Thus, it is clear that the U.S. has come a long way in terms of legalizing every eligible citizen's right to vote, but has a long way to go to make sure that paper promise becomes a reality.

Given the experience of Prairie View students and the actual potential for voter fraud, the question arises: Why should the Hip Hop Generation bother to vote if they face the possibility of intimidation and fraud at the ballot box? The answer to this question may vary from person to person, but three logical responses stand out.

One basic response involves the "bully on the playground" phenomenon. Imagine that at your school a ride on the playground slide is a highly prized activity. This is a grand slide with bumps and twists that produces much excitement and a rush of adrenaline. The problem with the slide is there are a lot of kids who want to ride, but there is only one hour for recess. If every kid who is entitled to a ride on the slide lines up, that means that there will be fewer opportunities for any one kid or select group of kids to enjoy the benefits of the slide. Realizing this dilemma, a bully will intimidate and harass the other children to prevent them from riding the slide so that he can realize a disproportionate share of value from the ride (i.e. he hogs the time and the resource for himself). The other children are prevented from getting their fair share of the ride's value.

The same lesson is true of the political process. The bully spends time intimidating and harassing people away from the ballot box because he wants to prevent many entitled citizens from realizing their fair share of the country's value. What is that value? Access to the levers of power that determines who controls trillions of dollars in tax-generated revenue, who receives society's wealth and who sets the rules by which society must live. Following the logic of the bully, therefore, the Hip Hop Generation must stand up and confront intimidation tactics at every turn by exercising their right to vote lest they be trampled on, disrespected, and powerless forever.

A second response argues that voting is a civic responsibility justified by the historical significance of the struggle to obtain the vote. It was less than 100 years ago that women and blacks were considered inferior beings not qualified to caste a ballot in U.S. elections. Prior to receiving the right to vote with the ratification of the 19th Amendment in 1920, women struggled for almost 100 years to achieve equal voting rights.[6] The African American struggle for voting rights has been even longer. When the Constitution was established in 1776, African Americans held as slaves were defined as three-fifths of a human being as a means of apportioning Congressional representation.[7] Following the Civil War, the U.S. ratified the 13th, 14th, and 15th Amendments which abolished slavery, established equal protection under the law for all people born or naturalized in the U.S., and gave African American men the right to vote respectively.[8]

Despite these constitutional "protections," it would take another 100 years or so of grassroots activism to guarantee these rights for African American men and women who faced discrimination at the ballot box and threat of injury or death prior to the passage of the Civil Rights Act of 1964 and the Voting Rights Act of 1965.[9] As a result of this long, hard-fought struggle for recognition and the ability to have a say in the way that they are governed, many African Americans recognize the right to vote as a birthright paid for by the blood, sweat, and tears of those who risked their lives to achieve equal rights in America. Under this reasoning, failing to vote dishonors the memory of those who sacrificed so that others, like the Hip Hop Generation, would have the right to do so.

The third reason most often cited is that younger people should vote because it affords them a measure of control over how their community is run. For example, many people complain about the courts and the types of decisions that judges make. Well, in most communities across the U.S., and at the federal level, judges are either appointed to office by elected officials or are elected by voters themselves. So if voters do not like the positions and decisions taken by judges they can either vote them out of office directly or lean on the representatives they elect to pass over those judges who do not hold the values that they deem important for office.

Whatever the rationale used for it, voting is an extremely important aspect of the political system in which we live. It is how we elect our representatives and is the foundation of the government that structures our lives. Electing the people who pick the judges, set the policies and distribute the money is a very important way that individuals and groups command power and respect in their communities. When individuals vote and join a bloc of voters who think like them, elected officials are forced to either defer to their desires before they make decisions or be held accountable by them after they make decisions. Fortunately, the process for registering to vote has gotten easier over time. While each state still maintains its own rules for voter registration, some include it in the drivers license application process and the federal government has created a national application form that can be used to register individuals from any state. Many community organizations seek to register voters at churches, schools, grocery stores, and local events.

The Hip Hop Generation should clearly understand that the act of voting is a two-step process. First, you must register to vote. There are many websites that allow you to fill out your voter registration application online and, depending on where you live, will provide information about where you can mail your application. Or, you can pick up the phone book and call your county elections office to get more information about how to register in your state. Second, and most importantly, you must actually vote. This can be accomplished by showing up at the polls to cast your ballot on election day or by filing an absentee ballot if you think that you will be out of town or otherwise unable to go to the polls on election day. Your county elections office will have more information about how to file an absentee ballot. The importance of actually voting cannot be ignored, as there is plenty of evidence that indicates many members of the H^2G register to vote but these same people fail to turn out at the polls on election day to cast their ballots. As a result, they miss out on many opportunities they have to shape and improve their communities from school and neighborhood elections to the many primary and general elections taking place at the city, state and federal levels.

Despite its importance, historical significance, and relative ease, voting remains one of the most contentious and misunderstood strategies for political participation. Ironically, the level of confusion about the role of the vote can be best understood through the clichéd arguments offered most often by those who do not vote. Statements like, "there's no difference between the candidates" and, "my one vote won't make a difference" are the most common. It is important for the H^2G to understand that the assumptions embedded in these arguments are fatalistic, disempowering and inaccurate in several respects. The first embedded assumption is that the vote is the only opportunity an individual has to influence an elected official. That once in office, there is nothing that can be done to hold the candidate accountable; the candidate is going to do what he or she wants to do regardless. So,

22

why bother? The rest of the book, which outlines multiple ways through which individuals can influence politicians, provides insight into why this particular assumption is incorrect.

The second embedded assumption is that the local election is the only race that matters. That there are no larger implications for the choices you make at the local level. The truth is, perhaps with the exception of local school board and city council elections, most politics is not all local. There is actually a larger game in town called party politics. The candidate you have the opportunity to select in your local election is most likely connected to a national party whose stance on policy issues and strategies for action can be quite meaningful for your life.

The following example attempts to provide a better understanding of what the vote represents in the political process. Let's say that politics is like a basketball game. The vote can be compared to the tip-off at the beginning of the game. Everyone who follows the game of basketball knows that the tip-off by itself does not win the team the game. It sets the stage for an early advantage and when used in coordination with other team tactics, like passing, free throws, and baskets, can eventually help tip the game in your team's favor.

Unlike basketball, however, the early advantage in politics does not last for seconds, minutes, or even four quarters. For example, in politics the advantage provided by the vote lasts for two years in the U.S. House of Representatives and four years for the Presidency. During this time, it is difficult for the team that lost the tip-off to maneuver on behalf of the policy issues important to the people, or constituents, they serve. The fact that the team you favor is disadvantaged can mean anything from the selection of judges who will not rule favorably on issues important to you to the redirection of funds to a community other than yours.

Now everyone wants to know that the team mate that they select to carry the ball can actually deliver a basket. The same is true for the candidate that you select. In order to determine if he or she makes the team you must evaluate several factors. First, determine the candidate's position on policy issues important to you. You can figure this out by talking to the candidate, examining voting records, listening to debate responses and reading the candidate's campaign literature. Second, you may want to size the candidate up by evaluating whether he or she is likely to do a good job in office. An examination of the candidate's professional track record, community service, family life, temperament, and conduct may help you determine whether he or she has what it takes to earn your vote.

These are a few important factors that should play into your decision to cast your vote for a candidate. So, next time an election comes up remember that you aren't voting for a candidate strictly as an individual, but also as a part of a larger team trying to win a policy game that has a direct impact on your life. Remember too that your vote, like the tip-off, isn't all that it takes to win the game. You need other tactics like those outlined in the following pages to help you press your advantage to a victory.

POINTS TO REMEMBER

1. Despite historic strides, voting fraud and abuse remains a reality today.
2. The H^2G must fight marginalization and exercise their right to vote.
3. Excuses for not voting are weak.
4. Voting allows individuals to exercise control over their lives and communities.
5. Be sure you do your homework before selecting candidates.
6. Register and Vote!

EASY STEPS TO VOTING IN U.S. ELECTIONS

1. You must be eligible to vote by being a U.S. citizen, at least 18 years of age by election day, and a resident of the city and state where you plan to cast your ballot.

2. You must register to vote before your state's deadline. A registration application can be filled out online at various websites (listed below). Registration applications may also be obtained at your local library, post office, or local elections office. Registration can also be completed while applying for services at locations such as the Department of Motor Vehicles or state public assistance offices. A voter registration card should be mailed to you prior to the elections.

3. Find out on what day the election takes place and determine whether you will be in town. If you will be out of town or otherwise unable to go to the polls on election, you should request an absentee ballot from your local election office and complete it prior to the state deadline.

4. Find out where you will vote on election day. Voters are required to cast their ballots at a polling place location determined by local election officials. You must contact the elections office or look on your voter registration card to determine where your polling place will be located.

5. Bring your voter registration card and a photo ID with you on election day. Election officials will ask you to verify your identity and sign in before allowing you to cast your ballot.

6. Request assistance if you are unfamiliar with the voting procedures, have a physical or reading impairment, or need a language interpreter. Most polling places provide a sample ballot and voting machine that you can view or practice on prior to going into the voting booth. Those who are impaired are allowed to take a friend or relative into the voting booth to provide assistance if they do not want help from the election officers.

7. Cast your ballot! Go into the voting booth and select the candidates of your choice.

(Re)SOURCES

Internet

Black Youth Vote   www.bigvote.org
(Learn about efforts to increase civic participation among young African Americans)

Capitol Advantage   www.capitoladvantage.com
(Locate a polling site near you, get your state's absentee ballot rules and other useful information)

Citizen Change   www.citizenchange.org
(Register to vote and find out what political activities P. Diddy has in store for the H^2G)

Federal Elections Commission   www.fec.gov
(Fill out an online voter registration form, learn when polls are open in your state, find out your state's deadline for voter registration)

Hip Hop Summit Action Network   www.hsan.org
(Get information on youth voter mobilization activities and the
involvement of the Hip Hop community)

League of Women Voters   www.lwv.org
(Get out the vote in your neighborhood with help from these women!)

NAACP National Voter Fund   www.naacpnvf.org
(Register to vote and learn about the issues)

Project Vote Smart   www.vote-smart.org
(Get informed about background, positions, and voting records of
candidates)

Rock the Vote/Rap the Vote   www.rockthevote.com
(Find out about voter suppression on college campuses and get
informed about issues)

Your Vote Matters   www.yourvotematters.org
(Register to Vote or Volunteer)

Youth Vote Coalition   www.youthvote.org
(Find out about efforts to train and inform young people about civic
participation)

Books

Brown, Adrian M. and William Upski Wimsatt. How To Get Stupid
    White Men Out of Power: The Anti-Politics, Unboring Guide
    to Power. Soft Skull Press, Inc. 2003.

"They say money's the root of all evil but I can't tell
YouknowhatImean, pesos, francs, yens, cowrie shells, dollar bills
Or is it the mind-state that's ill?"
Mos Def and Talib Kweli, "Thieves In the Night." <u>Black Star</u>.
Rawkus/Universal (1998)

Verse 2: More Money, More Power!

Since 1965, African Americans have primarily defined political
participation almost solely in terms of the vote. Many believe that if
you register to vote and cast your ballot, you have performed your
civic duty while doing what you could to influence the political
process. While voting remains an extremely important form of
political participation, there are other equally important—and highly
underutilized—ways to exert political influence.

Fundraising is one tactic that has become very influential in
contemporary politics. So much so, that there has been growing
concern about the influence of wealthy individuals and corporations in
the political process. Champions of the McCain-Feingold campaign
finance reform bill—passed by Congress and signed into law by the
President in 2001—claimed this legislation would reduce the role of
certain types of contributions in the political process at the federal
level. Despite these claims, many experts have noted that the
legislation has not reduced the influence of wealthy contributors—it
has only succeeded in shifting how the dollars flow through the
system. So, legislation and rhetoric notwithstanding, money continues
to be an important aspect of politics and it's time that folks realize it.

The reality is that just as our religious institutions need our
contributions to keep their doors open, our political institutions need
our financial support to maintain their viability and integrity. Elected
officials spend a significant amount of time fundraising so that they
can run for reelection and contribute to Political Action Committees,
or PACS, that help reelect other like-minded candidates who support
their policy goals. Experts acknowledge that candidates' reliance on
money has increased as the cost of running for and staying in office
has skyrocketed in recent years. To be elected to office in today's
society, a serious candidate has to have access to television, radio, and

print media outlets as well as costly campaign materials and, in many cases, expensive consultants.

Thus, it is important to realize that the candidates who work for issues of importance to you operate in a system where money matters. Money affects their ability to be elected, to wield influence among their peers, and to ultimately provide the resources needed to address important social and economic concerns in our communities.

Perhaps not surprisingly, minority candidates and political institutions often suffer financially, not because there is a lack of money among their natural constituents but because their communities have not been educated to understand why it is important to make political contributions. African Americans and Hispanics, for example, have not yet established a national grassroots infrastructure through which they can harness the power of their contributions—small or large—to support their political candidates and institutions. Interestingly enough, many experts note that if these groups fail to create and sustain their own political financial networks, other groups or parties with interests antithetical to the values and concerns of minority populations may wield more influence and power over their fates.

The good news is that awareness about this important aspect of the political process has been increasing among young people as the following example illustrates. In October 2000, a group of 20 and 30 something African Americans in Washington, D.C. decided that they wanted to make a difference in the presidential elections. Many of them were familiar with the political process as a result of working in and around Capitol Hill and understood the importance of having a financial impact. Calling themselves, Young Blacks for Gore (YB4Gore), 20 group members formally organized and decided to hold a fundraiser as one of their first activities. The group found a band, a venue, and a keynote speaker then issued invitations to their friends, families and co-workers. The evening of the event, many young black professionals attended having contributed modest amounts toward the fundraiser. The event was a success and eventually raised the original $20,000 target goal that the members had set.

30

The moral of this story could lie in the fact that the group's target goal was met by obtaining a large number of relatively modest contributions from within the African American community. However, the impact of the group's endeavors didn't end with the fundraising event. Working with Congressman William Jefferson and officials at the Democratic National Committee, group members leveraged their fundraising activity to launch a Get Out The Vote (GOTV) campaign targeting younger African Americans. Through an electronic advocacy campaign and an on-the-ground effort that placed many group members in key states on election day, the group's efforts provided a good example of how young people can organize and take positive action by using fundraising as a method for influencing the political process.

The H^2G can use fundraising as an effective tool to exert influence either by directly helping select candidates or by contributing to an organization or PAC that supports like-minded candidates or issues. There are several steps that the H^2G can take to organize a successful fundraising event.

1. *Determine the general political goal of the fundraising event.* Do you want to support a specific candidate, organization or PAC? If you want to support a candidate, is that person a member of a political body at the local, state, or federal level? Is he or she working for an issue or policy goal important to you and your community?

2. *Recruit other reliable individuals who share your objective to join a fundraising host committee.* You should make sure that these individuals are committed to raising funds from the people in their sphere of influence. Also, it is important to establish a governance structure by identifying a host committee chair and co-chair.

3. *Specify the parameters of your fundraising event.* What is your fundraising goal? Do you wish to raise $500, $5,000 or $50,000? Once this figure is set, then host committee members can split the figure evenly and take responsibility for raising their share. Committee members also must specify to whom the checks are to be made out. Usually a candidate will have a specific campaign name and contributions must be written accordingly. Finally, committee members must pre-determine if the event will include expenses like food, drink, or set up costs that must be covered. If so, discuss in advance how you will pay for these expenses. Will you set up a separate fund or use a percentage of the event proceeds to cover the event expenses? At all times financial transactions should be kept above board and subject to the sunshine rule (all business out in the open for review). You wouldn't want to spoil your reputation or the reputation of those associated with the event because of shady transactions.

4. If you decide to give to a candidate at the local, state, or federal level, *make sure that your fundraising is guided by the corresponding laws or regulations that may place limits on how much an individual or corporation can contribute to your event.* For example, the Federal Election Commission (www.fec.gov) regulates contributions to federal elected officials.

5. *Locate an appropriate venue.* The size of the venue should be determined by the amount of people the host committee expects to attend. Many restaurants or clubs with bars will allow you to hold your event at their facility for free in exchange for the proceeds for a cash bar. It is important to take these considerations when selecting a venue.

6. *Identify a keynote speaker and/or entertainment.* This will help draw a crowd. Most people do not like to give something for nothing—even if they know it is going toward a good cause. You should try to obtain the speaker or entertainer for free to keep event costs low. The politician that you are holding the fundraiser for is the most likely keynote speaker.

7. *Print and distribute invitations with solicitation cards enclosed.* Individual host committee members can be responsible for getting invitations to their target contributors. The invitations should contain the specifics of the event (including to whom the checks should be made) and should have inserts that allow those that cannot attend the event an opportunity to mail their contributions.

8. *Hold the event!* It is best for host committee members to collect their checks prior to the event and it is important to insist on checks—not cash—should you decide to accept contributions at the door. It is always nice for the fundraising event to be the culmination, not the beginning, of the actual money collection effort. There is nothing worse than trying to chase down host committee members for their obligations after the event has concluded.

9. Make sure all event debts are retired and send the contributions to the intended recipient.

These are a few steps that can set the H^{2}G on the right path toward becoming politically empowered by using fundraising as a tool for political participation. While much work needs to be done to establish a national fundraising infrastructure for disempowered communities, individual contributions and fundraisers remain important to the process and these efforts will certainly be effective in moving the H^{2}G towards their policy goals.

POINTS TO REMEMBER

1. Money matters in the U.S. Political system.
2. Candidates that you like need your financial support if they are to be effective and stay in office.
3. Many small contributions can make a big difference.
4. Young people can and should organize political fundraisers.
5. These fundraisers can be successful with careful planning.

(Re)SOURCES

Internet
Federal Election Commission   www.fec.gov
(Get information about federal campaign finance law and examine
federal campaign contributions and spending)

Combined Federal/State Disclosure & Election Directory
                        www.fec.gov/pubrec/cfsdd/cfsdd.htm
(Get a directory of state offices required to disclose information about
contributions and spending)

Democracy Matters   www.democracymatters.org
(Learn about an NBA player's attempt to change the influence of
money in politics)

Fundrace   www.fundrace.org
(Find out who your neighbors give money to!)

Books
Muntz, John and Kathryn Muray. <u>Fundraising for Dummies</u>. Wiley,
        John & Sons, Inc.   2000.
Warwick, Mal. <u>How to Write Successful Fundraising Letters</u>. Wiley,
        John & Sons, Inc.   2001.

"You gotta go for what you know
Make everybody see, in order to fight the powers that be
Lemme hear you say..."
Public Enemy, "Fight The Power." <u>Fear of A Black Planet</u>. Def Jam (1990)

Verse 3: Fight The Power!

In the mid-1990's, I got a job working at Purdue University's Black Cultural Center (BCC) as a way to earn extra cash and socialize while attending graduate school. Despite its lofty-sounding name, the BCC was actually an old, cramped 1940s era house stuffed with a gaggle of African artifacts, original artwork, a library, administrative offices and a multipurpose space. Early in my tenure we learned that the BCC was contaminated with asbestos. While the University decided to conduct asbestos abatement, the students used this occasion as a catalyst for working towards a new Black Cultural Center that more appropriately reflected the honor and dignity of their history. In the face of University resistance, we organized a series of protests that included demands for a new cultural center. Several televised rallies, newspaper interviews and a sit-in later, University administrators granted us a meeting to discuss how to move forward on building a new BCC. Committees were established, a fundraising drive was held and today a spanking new Black Cultural Center sits several blocks from where the old center stood.

African Americans, women and other marginalized groups have long used the power of protest to achieve goals and/or to convey their views to politicians and the public. From diner sit-ins and marches during the Civil Rights era to campus demonstrations during Vietnam—and, most recently, anti-war marches in major cities in the U.S. and abroad, protest has been used as an effective and legitimate tool for shaping public perceptions about issues and, if utilized properly, influencing the behavior of those in power.

Consider the case of a protest organized by the Hip Hop Summit Action Network in June of 2002 when New York Mayor Michael Bloomberg announced plans to cut $1.2 billion in public education funds to help close the city's growing fiscal crisis. Concerned about the impact of the cuts to a school system already overburdened and underfunded, the Hip Hop Summit Action Network led by founder Russell Simmons and Dr. Benjamin Chavis Mohammed organized a demonstration rally that shut down the New York public school system for a day as students and celebrities took to the streets to highlight their criticism of the planned cuts. As a result of their protest actions, Mayor Bloomberg backed off of his threats to cut funds for the school. This rally and the resulting policy shift clearly showed the power and potential of the Hip Hop Generation as a force for influencing political decisions.

When carefully planned, strategically implemented protests can be an effective tool for influencing policy outcomes. Yet, if not strategically employed, or used too frequently, protests can lose their intended impact. The public and people in positions of power will tune out once a group's tactics become repetitive or predictable.

In addition, the stakes can be extremely high when engaging this form of political participation. Of all of the forms of political participation, protest can be considered one of the most dangerous. Not only do protestors risk going to jail, they are also susceptible to incurring bodily harm. In recent history, protestors have been sprayed with water hoses, pepper and tear gas, attacked by dogs, beaten with clubs and some have even been shot and killed. While lawsuits against the offending law enforcement officials can be launched, these cases are difficult to litigate, could take years to conclude, and may result in a court decision that may give little satisfaction.

Nevertheless, protest organizers should not let these risks get in the way of speaking out. There are a number of steps that organizers can take to reduce the risk of harm to participants while getting the desired message across. Effective planning is the first step towards reducing the risks to participants and having a successful protest event. If conducting a march or rally, most cities require that protestors obtain multiple permits to operate on any given day on public streets, squares or in front of buildings. Without the appropriate permissions from the local authorities, the police have license to disassemble the group— largely by any means they deem necessary.

To avoid conflicts that are likely to occur without the permits, organizers should take steps to make certain that they have fulfilled all municipal requests including completing the appropriate paperwork, meeting application deadlines and the like. Some organizers have even taken steps to meet with police and local officials prior to the event to coordinate on logistics. While some argue that this approach undermines the subversive impact of the protest, it could result in fewer conflicts as it keeps all parties in the loop as to the scope, nature, and intent of the event.

In order to have an effective protest at least three key strategic areas must be addressed. First, you must clearly outline your goals and objectives. Are you trying to stop an action you deem harmful to your community or are you trying to increase awareness about an issue deserving of more attention? Who is your intended audience? Is your purpose to influence politicians, educate the public, gain media attention, disrupt proceedings, or all of the above? Clearly understanding your event goals will help determine the tactics, speakers and even location you will use to maximize the impact of your protest event.

Second, you must identify the tactics that will best facilitate the goals of the protest. Public rallies and/or demonstration marches are some of the most common tactics used in the U.S. Requiring careful logistics planning, these methods are employed because they allow participants to gain attention by occupying spaces where their views and opinions can be showcased to the public through speeches and signs. In addition, the number of people who show up in support of the protest symbolizes how widespread these views and opinions are shared. Other protest tactics include placing posters, flyers or graffiti in locations that are likely to get significant public attention, conducting sit-ins or call-ins that disrupt the operations of institutions that protestors are seeking to influence, and planning strategic interruptions to meetings and events that have some relationship to the protest's goals. In addition to massive letter-writing campaigns, there are likely many new ways that protestors can use Internet technology to create interruptions and disruptions that are likely to get their point across to officials.

It is important to note that while protestors sometimes operate on the fringe of what is considered acceptable and proper in society, the line should be drawn at the use of violence or intimidation tactics that threaten violence. Reflecting the philosophy of Mahatma Gandhi before him, Martin Luther King was adamant about the use of non-violent protest as the best way to counter racial oppression in America. Through marches and sit-ins organized by King's Southern Christian Leadership Conference (SCLC), participants were able to get their point across to a national and international audience. Scenes of excessive state violence being used against innocent protestors captured the hearts and minds of people around the world and eventually the U.S. government was pressured to change its tactics and implement policies that would promote social, economic and political inclusion for African Americans.

Establishing an effective communication strategy is the third and final area that must be addressed if you are to have a successful protest. Two levels of communications should be considered. The first level should focus on establishing effective communication among protest organizers and potential participants. You can't plan a multi-city protest event if organizers in each location aren't engaged in the plans and tactics to be employed. The Internet, as a low-cost and effective option, can be one way to help overcome distance and efficiently communicate with your troops. The leaders of recent anti-war and anti-globalization protests used Internet technology to coordinate logistics for events to be held in cities around the globe.

Once the logistics are solidified, organizers should focus on effective ways to communicate the details of the event to potential participants. In Washington, D.C., where I live, organizers of International ANSWER plastered flyers on street signs and light poles in locations throughout the city. A communication strategy targeting the mass media is another way to increase the effectiveness of your protest. When newspapers, television and radio stations are primed to spotlight your event, the attention serves to amplify your message and publicize it to potential participants.

We cannot talk about the power of protest without revisiting the tactics of a previous generation of young activists. In 1961, the Baton Rouge police held a 20-year-old student in solitary confinement for 58 days for leading a civil rights protest near the campus of Southern

University. Also expelled from the university, that student faced severe penalties with potentially life-altering consequences for standing up for what he believed in. Turning lemons into lemonade, Weldon J. Rougeau went on to graduate from Loyola University and Harvard University School of Law. Now President of the Congressional Black Caucus Foundation, Weldon has turned adversity into a successful career in the corporate and nonprofit sectors that has been driven by his experience as a protest leader in the 60s, which reinforced his desire to challenge injustice.

While Weldon's story turned out well, history is full of examples of individuals and groups who have not fared so well as a result of the political stands they have taken. Abraham Lincoln, Martin Luther King, Malcolm X, Huey P. Newton, and Fred Hampton are just a few who have suffered or died prematurely as a result of their protest actions. Countless others fill the ranks of the injured, isolated, and imprisoned. If it had not been for their sacrifice, however, many of the opportunities we now take for granted may have never been achieved. For that, it is important that we never forget the power of protest.

POINTS TO REMEMBER

1. Plan effectively.
2. Select protest tactics.
3. Establish an effective communication strategy.
4. Hold the protest event or activity!

(Re)SOURCES
Internet

Protest.net   www.protest.net
(Search upcoming U.S. and international protests by city, issue, and date)

International Answer   www.internationalanswer.org
(Learn more about anti-war and anti-racism protest efforts)

Partnership for Civil Justice   www.justiceonline.org
(Get more information about a fund that works to eliminate discrimination and prejudice)

NAACP Legal Defense Fund and Educational Fund, Inc.
                                     www.naacpldf.org
(Get help in your fight against discrimination and injustice!)

Puerto Rican Legal Defense and Education Fund
                                     www.prldef.org
(Get help in your fight against discrimination and injustice!)

American Civil Liberties Union   www.aclu.org
(Join the fight for civil liberties in the U.S.)

Books
Fanon, Frantz. The Wretched of the Earth. Grove Press, 1965.
    Black Skin, White Masks. Reprint Edition, Grove Press. 1991.

Loewen, James W. Lies My Teacher Told Me: Everything Your
    American History Text Book Got Wrong. Touchstone, 1996.

Churchill Ward and Jim Vander Wall. 2002. The Cointelpro Papers:
    Documents From The FBI's Secret Wars Against Dissent in
    the United States. South End Press (Second Edition).

DVD

Dixon, Ivan (Director). The Spook Who Sat By The Door (Based on the book by Sam Greenlee). Monarch Home Video, January 2004.

Lee, Spike. A Huey P. Newton Story. January, 2004.
Malcolm X. Warner Studios, 2000.
(www.pbs.org/hueypnewton)

Tejada-Flores, Rick and Ray Tellas. The Fight in the Fields: Cesar Chavez and the Farmworkers Struggle. 1996.

43

"Beautiful minds grind, grind for the dollarin'
Whether dice scholarin' or white collarin'
We all taught hustle to prophet like Solomon"
Common, "The Hustle." <u>Electric Circus</u>. MCA (2002)

Verse 4: The Influence Hustle

Every year, thousands of people converge on Capitol Hill to visit members of Congress—all for the express purpose of making requests of their elected officials. When I started working on Capitol Hill, I recall marveling at all of the visitors who roamed the halls of Congress on a daily basis. After a while, I came to know these people by type: large groups with buttons were usually members of a union or associations; men and women in dark suits with clients in tow were most likely professional lobbyists; groups of kids were on their classroom field trips; casually dressed families were tourists on vacation. Sadly, very few of these people—I would estimate less than 5 percent—were people of color.

Out of all of these people, some of them were on the Hill to conduct the primary business of Washington, D.C. and many state houses across the country: lobbying. Whether you get paid for it or you do it for free because you feel passionately about an issue, lobbying—also called advocacy by nonprofit groups—is considered one of the primary methods by which corporations, associations, groups and individuals influence the decisions made by legislators. What is lobbying and why is it important?

Lobbying is the practice of exerting influence in the political process by using direct forms of communication to share your views and ideas with elected officials. The ultimate goal of lobbying is to get politicians to respond to requests by either appropriating money toward your cause, adopting your policy perspective, or selecting the judge you prefer.

Lobbying and advocacy can be performed by entities such as businesses, associations, governments, schools, and individuals. Corporations pour millions of dollars into lobbying every year in an attempt to influence policy decisions that could have a financial impact on their bottom-line. Although subject to rules and regulations that

44

limit the value of gifts they can provide, corporate lobbyists are infamous for their lavish spending on behalf of elected officials and their staff. Also extremely well paid, corporate lobbyists are noted for their impeccable grooming and designer gear. Indeed, an area in the Longworth House Office Building outside of the Ways and Means Committee (one of the most important committees on the Hill) has been nick-named "Gucci Gulch" in honor of the many well-dressed lobbyists shod in Gucci loafers who walk the halls.

In the U.S., local and state governments also lobby the Congress in an effort to secure resources and ensure that policies are written to favor their budgets and/or residents. Many state governments focus on issues where they have shared responsibilities for federal programs such as Medicaid, Medicare, Food Stamps, TANF, and the State Child Health Insurance Program (SCHIP) to name only a few. Universities also lobby Congress heavily in an attempt to obtain federal monies to construct buildings and create or sustain campus programs.

While in-person visits to Congressional offices are the primary tool used by these lobbyists, there are other forms of lobbying that are quite effective. Associations that have a well-defined position about policy issues seek to put pressure on legislators through office visits, letters, faxes, and emails among other forms of communication. Because it is the primary duty of politicians and their staff to respond to requests for meetings and to letters, this type of advocacy work can have more immediate results than activities such as voting or protests. Lobbying is different from the other forms of political activity primarily because much of the guesswork is taken out of the equation. Once the lobbyist has made contact, he or she has issued a specific request to a specific decision maker about a specific issue. Because of this direct request, policy makers cannot claim that they weren't asked, did not know or were not informed about the issue.

If you believe lobbying is the tactic that you or your group want to pursue—indeed it is the important and necessary first step for most political action strategies—then there are several things that you must consider to be an effective lobbyist.

First, target politicians in the appropriate political body at the appropriate level. There is nothing worse than wasting time making visits, phone calls and writing letters to politicians who do not have the power to affect your issue. For example, making a request of the mayor when the request should have been directed to members of the state legislature.

In order to know what political body and which governmental level to lobby, you must first do your homework to determine whether it's a local, state, or federal issue. If you determine your state or federal government has the most influence, you should then discover whether your efforts would be best spent working on the Senate and/or House/Assembly side of the legislative body. Finally, you should identify which committee within the legislative body has jurisdiction over, or power to affect, your issue. Once you have discovered the answer to these questions, then you should put on the full court press to make sure that your views are heard. Following these simple steps can save you valuable time, energy, and resources.

Second, you should make sure to craft your appeal. It is always best to figure out what form of communication will best convey the message that you are trying to amplify. Some professional lobbyists tailor their message for its intended audience. For example, using select buzzwords or phrases to spin your message may increase your intended target's receptivity. Some professional lobbyists have discovered that the messenger is often as important as the message content. For instance, if you are trying to sway policymakers on an issue related to veteran benefits you might maximize your influence if someone who has served in the military delivers the message. Whatever your method, it is important that you don't compromise your core objectives or values in your attempt to make your lobbying request appeal to diverse audiences.

As mentioned previously, African Americans do not yet have a sustained lobbying presence on Capitol Hill. While groups like the Leadership Conference on Civil Rights, the National Association for the Advancement of Colored People, the National Council of Negro Women, and the National Urban League have Washington operations that seek to provide ongoing policy input on issues ranging from how to shape welfare laws to the selection of federal judges, their presence is limited when compared to the host of the laws and issues relevant to the black community that should be raised and when compared to the near constant lobbying presence of other groups in Washington.

To their credit, the enterprising women of Delta Sigma Theta Sorority Incorporated don their crimson and cream outfits every year and arrive on Capitol Hill en masse to lobby Congress on issues of importance to African Americans. While their presence is impressive and necessary, more groups—including the Hip Hop community—need to make lobbying days a priority for their organizations.

Despite the enormity of the task at hand, however, the African American organizations that do have a lobbying effort often work in tandem to influence legislators thinking and votes on issues of very high importance and have had a number of victories—particularly in defeating the appointment of judges hostile to civil rights laws to the federal bench.

Surprisingly, one of the most effective black lobbying efforts that I witnessed while I worked on Capitol Hill did not come from the traditional Civil Rights organizations, but from Tom Joyner, the hardest working man in show business. Working with Tavis Smiley, Joyner's Morning Show has mobilized thousands of listeners to contact their members of Congress on issues ranging from HIV/AIDS to the treatment of Historically Black Colleges and Universities.

Not only have the switchboards of the Capitol been overwhelmed by Joyner fans who have been instructed to call Congress, Committee Chairs (who until their phones were flooded had no idea who Tom Joyner was)—have changed their actions and votes based on the aggressive call-in lobbying tactics of Morning Show listeners. Using a mix of humor, facts and persuasive argumentation, Tom and Tavis have helped to change the face of lobbying by creatively challenging black Americans to become active participants in the democratic process. Their efforts have made a positive difference.

Some may ask: What is the difference between lobbyists and those looking for a hand out? The answer: not much. When requests for resources come from or on behalf of those who are seen as society's undeserving, people hold their nose and call it welfare, but when the similar requests for assistance come from professionals in Brooks

Brothers suits or from other socially acceptable sources, it is referred to as lobbying.

It is important to realize that asking for what you want or need from the U.S. government is nothing to be ashamed of. It is not welfare. It is not charity. It is the democratic process at work. By letting those who represent you, and for whom you vote, know exactly how you feel and what you or your communities need from them, you are engaging in a fundamental and necessary principle of democracy.

POINTS TO REMEMBER

1. Do your homework to find out if your issue is decided at the local, state, or federal level.
2. Determine which political body is the most appropriate target.
3. Craft your appeal with a persuasive message or messenger.
4. Make your pitch!

(Re)SOURCES

Internet

Charity Lobbying in the Public Interest   www.clpi.org
(Link to lobbying strategies and resources that will advance the interests of charities)

Influence: The Business of Lobbying   www.influence.biz
(For those who want to know more about the professional lobbying business)

The Democracy Center   www.democracyctr.org/resources/lobbying
(Read detailed but easy to digest information about the basics of
lobbying)

THOMAS   http://thomas.loc.gov
(Research the legislation and votes passed in the U.S. Congress)

Books

Luneburg, William. The Lobbying Manual: A Compliance Guide for
    Lawyers and Lobbyists, 2nd Edition. American Bar
    Association. 1998.

Smucker, Bob. The Nonprofit Lobbying Guide: Second Edition.
    Independent Sector. 1999. (also available as a PDF at
    www.clpi.org/BOOK/nonprofitlobbyingguide.pdf)

Watkins, Michael et al. Winning the Influence Game: What Every
    Business Leader Should Know About Government. Wiley,
    2001.

"Take notes: real gangstas wear trench coats
Grey suits, black ties and they seek votes"
Ice-T, "Message to the Soldier." <u>Home Invasion</u>. Priority Records (1993)

Verse 5: Politicking for a Purpose

As a little girl, Alicia Reece recalls running around after her father Steve who served as a political aide to Theodore Berry, the first African American mayor of Cincinnati, Ohio. Exposed to politics at a young age, Alicia developed an interest in politics and how it could be used to empower communities. Despite her political upbringing, she wasn't interested in pursuing politics as a career when she enrolled in college at Grambling State University in Louisiana. A marketing major, Alicia involved herself in campus activities—including hosting a radio show on the university's radio station—content with the idea that she would one day open a marketing firm in her hometown of Cincinnati.

Then, in 1991, former Ku Klux Klan leader David Duke decided to run for governor of Louisiana. In the face of the Duke campaign and rumored proposals to turn Grambling into a state prison, Alicia organized a Get Out The Vote effort that successfully registered more than 7,000 new young voters. Upon returning to her hometown, Alicia pursued the marketing firm idea and worked in her family's business yet maintained her activism in the local political arena. After running a youth Get Out The Vote campaign for the Hamilton County Democratic Party, she was asked to serve as a community outreach director for the campaign of U.S. Rep. David Mann. It was during this time that she met U.S. Congresswoman Maxine Waters who became her political mentor. Observing Alicia in action, Congresswoman Waters told her that she should think about running for office and to call her in Washington when she got ready to run. Several years later, Alicia decided to run for a seat on the Cincinnati city council and called Maxine Waters who sent her a campaign contribution and returned to Ohio to help Alicia campaign. At the age of 28, Alicia ran for and won a seat on the Cincinnati city council. Within four years, she became the first and youngest African American woman elected to the position of Vice Mayor of the city of Cincinnati.

Running for office has long been considered one of the highest forms of public service. Indeed, most elected officials say they run for office because they want to make a difference in their communities or they want to serve their country. Yet, many younger people do not run for office because they believe that they will not be taken seriously, do not have enough established credentials, or do not stand a chance running against incumbents (the elected official who already holds the position). Nevertheless, Alicia's story illustrates that young people can and do win political office if they lay the proper groundwork and set their minds to accomplishing their goal. So, for those members of the Hip Hop Generation who have fresh ideas and believe that they have a lot to offer, there is no reason why running for office should not be a serious consideration.

Becoming an elected official is one of the highest forms of political empowerment because a person in the position can wield a significant amount of influence that can be used to make a difference in the community. As mentioned previously, elected officials control the levers of government that determine the flow of trillions of dollars in taxpayer funds. Elected officials influence how people in communities live their lives by shaping legislation that can change existing law or create new laws. Elected officials help determine the scope and depth of important programs and services for the community and many appoint the judges who run the justice systems at the federal, state and local levels. In essence, elected officials regulate the behavior of corporations, organizations, states, communities, individuals, and even nations through the policies that they shape.

It is because of the significant power that elected officials possess, that these entities line up outside of their doors in the hopes of influencing their thinking about a multitude of issues both domestic and international. Because they are highly sought after, elected officials also receive many perks in the forms of trips, dinners, receptions, and gifts. Given the amount of power and perks that come with the office, it is no wonder that many incumbents stay in office for a long time and are loath to lose their seats to challengers.

In the modern political arena where money and the media reign supreme, there are several things that the H^2G should consider before making a bid for office. First, have you identified and established a political base that can help you win? Most political aspirants have built a base of core supporters who are familiar with them and willing to lend their talent, energy, and financial contributions to their campaigns. Perhaps you are active in your church, are a member of a community association, or have exhibited community leadership in other ways. The people who got to know you as a result of your membership or activism can be your staunchest supporters and you should be able to call upon them to make up your political base.

Second, do you have a well-defined reason for why you want to run for office, or better still, why others should vote for you? Is there something that the current elected official isn't doing that you feel that you could do better? What are the specific policies or issues that will comprise your political platform? Is there a need in the community that has been overlooked? Each of these questions must be carefully considered prior to announcing your intentions publicly. The strength of your answers to these questions can help determine the strength of your campaign.

Which brings us to qualifications, a third consideration you must take into account prior to launching your candidacy. Qualifications are usually the first set of assets the public assesses when an individual declares their candidacy. While this is an area that traditionally disadvantages younger candidates who tend to have less professional experiences to draw upon, it is a hurdle that can be overcome by taking an honest inventory of the type of work that you have done, the level of responsibility that you have undertaken in various organizations and crafting an appeal that leans heavily on character and substantive policy issues. Often individuals who are considered most qualified are those who have experience in the community, so do not discount activities such as membership in church or youth groups. You may be surprised at how responsive the public can be to a fresh face who has been active in the community and who has energy and good ideas.

A fourth item you must consider when running for political office is does your personal life lend itself to public scrutiny? Politics can be a dirty business. Many incumbents who fear losing their power and influence are not afraid to use "opposition research" to dig up information about you or your family. As a result, the politics of personal destruction can be employed as a tactic to derail your candidacy. To protect yourself from some of these underhanded strategies, it is important that you take inventory of your past and that of your close family members when making your decision to run for office. If you identify a potential issue, but decide to move ahead anyway, make sure that you devise a response strategy should your opponent decide to highlight this issue during the campaign.

Next, have you determined how much it will cost to launch your campaign? Most candidates are not independently wealthy and while some may use their personal money to start the campaign, they then rely on contributions from supporters to finance the bulk of their campaign expenses. The costs of campaigns vary depending on the type and level of office and whether there is a primary and general election. The bulk of campaign expenses are taken up by costly television, radio and print advertisements as well as campaign literature and paid staff. In today's media driven environment, each of these factors are important for maximizing a candidates exposure and his or her ability to reach the public.

A sixth consideration is establishing a party affiliation. Most candidates run on a Republican or Democratic ticket, or ballot, although more are aligning with smaller parties like the Green Party or even running as Independents. The question of party affiliation is an important one for several reasons. Many in the public use party identification as a mental shortcut for understanding what issues you are likely to stand for. For example, Democrats are generally associated with a policy platform that allows women the right to choose an abortion while Republicans are usually portrayed as taking the opposite position. Green Party candidates are most often considered pro-environment. Of course, these shortcuts don't always hold true, as there are some Democrats who are pro-life just as there are some Republicans who are pro-choice. Party affiliation is also important because you have a potential base of ready voters who self-identify with the party and who are more likely to vote for you because of your affiliation. Finally, party identification can be important because it can also mean increasing your access to party resources like phone banks, volunteers, and donor lists. All of these things are important for launching a successful campaign.

A final consideration is that it is important to establish a formal campaign structure with a campaign manager, scheduler, fundraising consultant, and press secretary. Having a formal campaign structure brings a level of professionalism to your campaign and reduces the likelihood of major gaffes like missed filing deadlines or fundraising violations. In addition, a professional campaign structure conveys how serious you are about your candidacy and makes your campaign more appealing to donors who aren't keen on giving money to an ineffective operation. Prevailing logic dictates that if you can run a professional campaign you have what it takes to run a professional political office.

Younger Americans are increasingly stepping up to the plate to run for political office. You may have heard of Kwame Kilpatrick, the 32 year old Mayor of Detroit or Harold Ford Jr. who was 27 when he first joined the U.S. House of Representatives. But have you heard of Corey Booker of Newark, New Jersey or Craig Watkins of Dallas, Texas? Most likely you have not because both of these young men, running for mayor of Newark, New Jersey and district attorney for Dallas County, Texas respectively, lost their bid for office. Despite their losses, both candidates gave their well-established opponents a run for their money and came so close to winning that many people predict they will prevail in the next elections. The Booker and Watkins examples provide excellent insight into how young African Americans have the ability to launch professional campaigns. And, even though they lost, these individuals likely served as an inspiration to others and are well positioned to have bright political futures.

(Re)SOURCES

Internet

Campaign for Young Voters   www.campaignyoungvoters.org
(Gives advice and information to candidates about how to target young voters)

Congressional Black Caucus Political Leadership and Education Institute   www.cbcinstitute.org
(Campaign training for African Americans seeking to become campaign staff and/or run for office)

Emily's List   www.emilyslist.org
(Campaign training and assistance for women running for elected office)

National Women's Political Caucus   www.nwpc.org
(Campaign training and issue advocacy for women and families)

The White House Project   <u>www.thewhitehouseproject.org</u>
(Get training and issue information from a group trying to place the first female President in the White House)

Books

Gruber, Susan. <u>How To Win Your 1st Election</u>. CRC Press, Second
     Edition, 1997.

Thomas, Robert J. and Doug Gowen. <u>How to Run for Local Office:
     A Complete Step-By-Step Guide That Will Take You Through
     The Entire Process of Running and Winning a Local Election</u>.
     R&T Enterprises, Inc. 1999.

Verse 6: The Freebie Force

O.K. So perhaps you are attracted to the energy and excitement of a political campaign, but feel that running for office is not for you. Volunteering on a campaign can be just as important and rewarding as actually running for office.

I volunteered for my first campaign when I was a 19-year-old sophomore at Prairie View A&M University in Texas. One of my professors, Dr. Hulen Davis, decided to run for Waller County Commissioner and asked me—at the time President of Prairie View's Political Science Club—to coordinate his campaign. While I had never run a campaign before, I thought it would be good experience to add to my resume and accepted the challenge. I got a group of my friends together and we set out to put a campaign structure and message together that would convince P.V. students that Davis was the man for the job. Davis's opponent was a man named Frank Jackson who also worked at Prairie View. Popular, younger and well-liked by students, Jackson had a charisma and a compelling message that attracted many to his campaign. In the end, despite our best efforts, Jackson won the race and while I was disappointed that my candidate lost, I learned invaluable lessons about the inner workings of a political campaign.

Campaign volunteers serve a vital role in the functioning of a political campaign and can be the key to the success or failure of a candidate. Cash-strapped candidates rely on volunteers to do tasks like disseminating campaign materials, stuffing envelopes for mass mailings, making phone and house calls to local residents and writing press releases and issue briefs. Because a candidate relies on all of these activities to communicate with the electorate, a dearth of volunteers or volunteers of poor quality can result in a lost election.

Imagine what would happen if a campaign manager instructed volunteers to leaflet a neighborhood in a key voting area, but the volunteer, tired of working, dropped the leaflets in the trash instead?

The candidate would have wasted precious money on printing the leaflets and, worse, his or her message would have been lost on voters in this area. This missed opportunity to connect with voters would also most likely be reflected in the voting returns for that precinct on Election Day.

Since resources are especially tight during an election, it is very important that candidates attract bright, talented, energetic and dedicated volunteers. If volunteering is attractive to you there are several qualities you must possess in order to receive maximum benefit from the experience. First, it is a good idea to volunteer for a candidate with whom you share common policy goals and political philosophies. Since you are not getting paid for your time, it is important that you are motivated to do a good job for other reasons like admiring the candidate's work in the community or believing strongly in the candidate's policy ideas. This link will sustain you during long hours of hard and often tedious work. It will also be the driving force behind your motivation to do a good job and will likely lead to your efforts being noticed by the candidate.

You must also be willing to sacrifice your free time. Campaign needs are 24 hours, seven days per week. Whether answering phones, posting signs, or driving the candidate around, there is always something that needs to be done. As a result, it is possible to spend almost every waking moment at campaign headquarters—especially during the final days leading up to the election.

Next, you should do everything in your power to recruit your friends and family members to help with the campaign. Because there are so many things to be done, it is helpful to the campaign to have many hands on deck to perform the exhaustive tasks that must be completed. Bringing your network of family and friends into the loop could make the experience more enjoyable for you and it would impress the candidate who should be appreciative of your dedication.

Finally you must be willing to be flexible. Even though you may have specialized skills or an advanced degree that would make you a perfect fit to work in a designated area such as media relations or campaign finance, you must be prepared to get in where you fit in, do the unexpected, and help out with whatever pressing tasks need to be completed. If you are the type of person that has a problem pitching in and performing menial tasks like stuffing envelopes and answering phones, then you should probably rethink becoming a campaign volunteer.

If you think you possess all of these qualities, then volunteering on a campaign could be for you. There are a number of benefits that could result from your hard work. Volunteering on a campaign could plug you into a formidable network of influential people. It could expose you to an array of issues that could significantly expand your knowledge base, expand your skills and give you valuable work experience that you could list on your resume. Finally, volunteering can lead to a job for you or a lucrative career if your candidate should win office.

I have met many Congressional staffers who have received job offers as a result of volunteering on political campaigns. Many have risen to hold positions of importance in the elected official's office. As a result of the exposure and skills developed in these positions, some have even gone on to establish lucrative, high profile careers in business and government.

The important thing to remember is that you never know what doors may be opened to you as a result of volunteering on political campaigns. It is for this and the other reasons listed above that you should put your best foot forward if you decide to donate your time and energy to a campaign.

POINTS TO REMEMBER

1. Volunteer for a candidate with whom you share common values and ideas.
2. Be willing to commit a good chunk of your free time.
3. Recruit friends and volunteers to help out.
4. Be flexible enough to handle a variety of duties.
5. Use your volunteer experience to network.
6. Do a good job!

(Re)SOURCES

Internet

Action Without Borders   www.Idealist.org
(Learn about volunteer opportunities by country, state, city and area of interest)

21st Century Democrats   www.21stcenturydems.org
(Provides volunteer and training opportunities for progressive-leaning individuals)

Contact major political parties to learn about volunteer opportunities!

The Democratic Party   www.Democrats.org
         202-863-8000

The Green Party   www.GreenParty.org
         1-866-GREENS2

The Libertarian Party   www.lp.org
         1-800-ELECTUS

The Republican Party   www.rnc.org
         202-863-8500

Reform Party   www.reformparty.org
         1-800-GO-REFORM

Your Vote Matters   www.yourvotematters.org
(Sign up to volunteer on election day!)

Books

Jee, Kim et al. Future 500: Youth Organizing and Activism in the United States. Subway and Elevator Press. 2002.

Kielburger, Marc and Craig Kielburger. Take Action: A Guide To Active Citizenship. Wiley, 2002.

Wallenius, Dale. Get Up, Get Out, And Volunteer! A Simple Book That Will ChangeYour Life. Iuniverse, Inc. 2003.

Verse 7: Working 4 the (Wo)Man

There are a number of pathways that the Hip Hop Generation can take to establish a career in the political arena. Many of the professional staff members I met while working on Capitol Hill received their jobs by volunteering on a political campaign. However, a significant number also received their first exposure to the possibility of a career through internship and fellowship opportunities. Whatever the path, every year legions of young people descend on Washington, DC and state houses across the country to work in political offices as paid staff, fellows or interns.

My own career in the political arena started when I received an opportunity to work on Capitol Hill as a Congressional Black Caucus Foundation Legislative Fellow in the fall of 1997. Assigned to the office of Congressman Melvin Watt of North Carolina, I worked as a Legislative Assistant analyzing policies related to Medicare, Medicaid, Social Security and women and children.

While researching a Social Security issue, I came into contact with the Director of the Social Security Subcommittee of the powerful House Ways and Means Committee--a woman named Sandy Wise-- who hired me to work on Social Security issues full time after my fellowship period ended. I was in this position when I met Congressman Charles Rangel, a founding member of the Congressional Black Caucus, Dean of the New York State Congressional Delegation and Ranking Member of the House Ways and Means Committee. Responsible for providing him with briefings, updates and other information, the exposure that I received from this position prompted Congressman Rangel to approach me about working for him as his Chief of Staff approximately nine months later. So, at the age of 27, I left the Ways and Means Committee to become the youngest and longest-serving female Chief of Staff to the Honorable Charles B. Rangel of Harlem, New York. My years on Capitol Hill gave me critical experience and opened a world of opportunities previously unimagined. I gained policy expertise, administrative experience, tremendous networking opportunities, new travel experiences, and better insight into the political process as a result of the work that I did.

From my experiences on the Hill, I learned that working as professional staff for a politician can be demanding, but also fun and rewarding if you are passionate about issues and seeking a way to have some influence in the policymaking process. Depending on your educational background and interests, a job working for an elected official can include anything from drafting legislation, answering constituent mail and preparing issue briefs to scheduling appointments, meeting with lobbyists and supervising office staff. Whether your position is administrative, policy-related or a combination of both, working in a political office can be a very enriching educational experience that can have a lasting impact on your life and career.

It is, in part, because of this significant educational opportunity that many younger people pursue professional staff positions in the political arena. There are, however, a few additional reasons why working for an elected official can promote political empowerment. The first is the unusual amount of influence that staffers can wield as a result of their proximity to the elected official. Because of the sheer amount of issues to be considered by an elected official at any given time, the number of people pulling at their coattails, and the limited amount of time to consider all of the issues and conduct their officials duties, most elected officials rely heavily on their staff in order to get their jobs done. Out of necessity, therefore, staffers become an extension of the elected official and oftentimes act as a surrogate. Thus, idealistic staffers who want to make a difference in their communities can actually help shape important policy decisions because of the level of influence they hold in an elected official's office.

They can also take advantage of many of the perks that come with the territory. For example, many lobbyists try to influence the opinion of staffers as a way to try to influence the elected official's thinking on an issue. This results in perks for staff such as gifts, dinners, seminars and trips sponsored by lobbyists. These staffers must take care to observe the rules and regulations that govern the receipt of these perks for a violation can result in a reprimand or a dismissal that can effectively destroy their political careers.

Many political staffers also become experts on important policy issues that the elected official is too busy to master. Expertise, therefore, is a second way that professional staff can become empowered by working in an elected official's office. When a staffer learns the ins and outs of obscure policy details, he or she is sought after for their knowledge and ability to discern where and how laws need to be changed. Of course, this knowledge also allows staff experts to make a difference in the community by suggesting and working towards changes that can improve lives and neighborhoods. Serving in an elected official's office, therefore, can be quite an effective form of community service.

Many in the Hip Hop Generation are not familiar with or do not know how to gain access to the job opportunities that are available in the political arena. Internships and fellowships provide a good way to learn about the many opportunities available at all levels and in all branches of government.

There are a number of organizations that work with local, state, and federal political institutions to coordinate internship placements for high school and undergraduate students. Internships are often unpaid temporary jobs that allow students to work in the office of an elected official for two to three months in the summer, spring or fall months. Once assigned to an office, interns perform duties such as opening mail, answering phones, drafting basic letters, and running errands in an effort to learn the inner-workings of a political office environment. While interns are often the lowest people on the totem pole in the office hierarchy, they complete vital tasks that are important to the functioning of the elected official's office.

If you are a graduate student, professional student or mid-career professional, there are also a number of enriching fellowship opportunities that will increase your exposure to the policy world. Fellowships are different from internships in several respects. First, a fellow is usually assigned to an elected official's office for longer periods of time such as nine months starting in the spring, fall or winter. Second, fellowships are usually paid positions that are funded by a sponsoring Foundation or non-profit organization. And, third, fellows are most often assigned heavier responsibilities in an elected official's office due to their higher education level. As a result, fellows usually serve as temporary policy staff responsible for duties such as: helping the elected official understand complex issues, responding to constituent mail, and preparing questions for hearings and/or speeches for the elected official's speaking engagements.

Whatever type of experience you seek, most internship and fellowship programs have similar application requirements that can be highly competitive. These applications often require basic contact information, a copy of your high school, undergraduate, or graduate school academic transcripts, and personal statements expressing why you are interested in the opportunity. If you pass the paper test, some will even follow up with a telephone or in-person interview as a way to determine their list of finalists. Because many of these programs are highly competitive and some are even paid, it is imperative that great care is taken to produce a well-thought-out, quality application.

Many fellows and interns who are interested in landing permanent jobs in politics capitalize on the connections that they make while working in their internship or fellowship assignments. Recall that it was connections that I made while serving as a Congressional Black Caucus Legislative Fellow that enabled me to launch a career in the political arena. There are many other staffers on Capitol Hill that I met who owe their careers to fellowship or internship opportunities they received.

It is possible for the H^2G to land political jobs without having had internship or fellowship experience. It can be as easy as writing, calling, or visiting the office of an elected official to inquire about the availability of positions. However, since many will ask for relevant previous work experience, it would be beneficial if you attempted to land an internship, fellowship, or campaign volunteer experience prior to applying for a permanent position. Having these experiences under your belt will also help you test the waters to determine if working in a political office is really for you.

A final word of caution: Like most jobs, while the benefits and perks of a political job may be considerable, there are downsides that can lessen the pleasurable and rewarding aspects of the experience. Because elected officials often have extremely busy schedules that require them to be "on" from very early in the morning to very late at night, many also need their staff to keep long hours. Staff provides them with the support that they need to conduct meetings, keep abreast of pressing legislative issues, and make speeches, among many other activities. Depending on the style and needs of your elected official, therefore, the hours can be extremely long. Needless to say, this type of rigorous environment can create an unhealthy imbalance between your professional and personal life and the stress can even take a toll on your health if you let it.

Another infrequent, but unpleasant aspect of the job can include the negative personality quirks of some elected officials. Some are known to treat their staff with extreme disrespect—often employing behaviors that are considered rude, intimidating and mean. Fortunately, others in the political arena are often familiar with the reputation of these officials and can help you steer clear if you ask before you apply for a job. If for some reason you find yourself working for a politician with a personality deficit, do not hesitate to find another position with one of the many elected officials who respect the work of the team of professionals who make it possible for them to do their jobs effectively. There is no reason why you should take verbal, physical, or psychological abuse in your quest to make a difference in your community.

(Re)SOURCES

Internet

Asian Pacific American Institute for Congressional Studies
www.aipac.org
(Provides internship and fellowship opportunities for Asian-Pacific Island undergraduate and graduate students)

Congressional Black Caucus Foundation   www.cbcfinc.org
(Provides internship and fellowship opportunities for African American high school (DC only), undergraduate, graduate and professional students)

Congressional Hispanic Caucus Institute   www.chci.org
(Learn about internship and fellowship opportunities for Latino undergraduate and graduate students)

Looksmart   www.looksmart.com
(Type in "Congressional Internships" and get a listing of over 300 opportunities!)

The Politix Group   www.politixgroup.com
(Provides an overview of the careers in politics and government as well as contact information for a host of political and government job opportunities)

USA Jobs   http://www.usajobs.opm.gov/
(Search for jobs in the federal government by location, agency, job category and salary)

U.S. House Employment Office   http://www.house.gov/cao-hr/
                                   202-225-2450
(Search for employment opportunities in the House of Representatives)

U.S. Senate Employment Office   www.senate.gov
(Apply for a job in a Senate office) 202-228-JOBS

White House Office of Presidential Personnel
https://sawho04.eop.gov/cgi-bin/appointments
(Apply for a political position in the White House or Executive Branch)

Books
Rubinstein, Ellen. <u>Scoring a Great Internship</u>. Natavi Guides 1st Edition, 2002.

72

"Tomorrow, our seeds will grow
All we need is dedication"
Lauryn Hill, "Everything Is Everything." The Miseducation of Lauryn Hill.
Sony (1998)

Verse 8: Networking Power

Have you ever seen the behavior of crabs that have been placed in a barrel? All want desperately to get out of the barrel yet when one crab looks as if it is getting further than the rest, the others reach up to pull it down to their level. As a result, none of the crabs ever get high enough to escape from the barrel. It is this "crab at the bottom of the barrel" mentality that pervades the thinking of many individuals and undermines the success of our communities.

A close cousin to the crab mentality is the "I've got mine, so you get yours the best way you can" attitude. In this formulation, a single crab has managed to get to the top of the barrel, but instead of sharing strategies for success with his or her fellow crabs, the triumphant crab remains the only species of its kind in a high position. While it's nice to have a successful crab in the family, without putting mechanisms in place to help others reach high positions, the single crab's success will make no difference for the liberation of the crab community—still stuck at the bottom of the barrel.

In either scenario, the success of the community depends on working together in a way that allows all members to be lifted out of the barrel. In this formulation, individuals pursuing a path of upward mobility share a common interest in reaching back to give a hand up to others even as they climb toward success. In addition, organizations and groups that are working toward a common goal form partnerships and coalitions that draw upon their collective strengths to achieve shared objectives. Great strategists like George Fraser and Dennis P. Kimbro call this approach networking: linking people and organizations together in ways that create a human and institutional chain of connections that can help advance individual and community success.

If one were to look back on history at every major social advancement in the U.S. over the past century and a half, they would

73

find that these accomplishments depended upon the hard work of a collective group of individuals and organizations that formed coalitions—the ultimate networking strategy—to achieve their social goals. For example, the Civil Rights Movement depended upon the strategic tactics of various individuals such as Martin Luther King, Fannie Lou Hamer, Bayard Rustin, A. Philip Randolph, Dorothy Height, Roy Wilkins, Thurgood Marshall, Whitney Young, Walter Fauntroy, John Lewis and Julian Bond and organizations such as the Student Nonviolent Coordinating Committee, the Southern Christian Leadership Conference, the NAACP, the Urban League, and the National Council of Negro Women. Given the complexity of the issues to be addressed and the multiple tactics that will need to be employed, it is likely that the Hip Hop Generation will have to undertake a similar collective approach in order to achieve important political and policy priorities.

The role of the dedicated individual should not be ignored in the networking equation. When individuals in positions of power possess a collective "we" philosophy, they are able to work in tandem with others to advance a larger agenda. Yet, too often, just like the crabs, individuals or groups get into power and they have no allegiance to anyone other than themselves. And, even though their opportunities may have been built on the shoulders of others, they refuse or are incapable of understanding their role and responsibility to help others. This "me" mentality is particularly troublesome because positions of power usually bring with them great resources and expanded opportunities to change or influence the status quo. Unfortunately, there are too many examples of individuals who have achieved great success who exist in self-centered silos that prevent them from working with others in a manner that promotes collective empowerment.

It is important to note that government officials are not the only people who wield power in our society. There are others such as business executives, religious leaders, entertainers, and sports figures that also carry great influence that can be parlayed into political power. Thus, it is essential for the H^2G to understand that placing the right people—those who realize the importance of collective action—in key positions so that they can help further the cause is an important and necessary ingredient for political empowerment strategies. The H^2G will also have to fight against the prevailing "me" impulse in contemporary society and cultivate a "we" consciousness. Yet this can only occur if individuals shed the disabling attitudes that prevent them from linking together in ways that enable the pursuit of a political or ideological checkmate.

The same crippling situation holds true for organizations. There are a multitude of examples of organizations failing to work together to maximize their resources to bring about the common good. An unfortunate example of this phenomenon can be found in religious institutions located in impoverished communities. With millions of dollars flowing through their coffers every Sunday morning, the churches are the most resource rich institutions in these communities. The sheer magnitude of resources that churches generate could be magnified tenfold if they were to join together to serve as catalysts for positive and widespread change in their communities. For example, if churches in a city or region were to link up with each other and pool a certain percentage of their revenue, they would be able to create community investment funds that could spur neighborhood redevelopment, job opportunities, and poverty reduction programs on a large scale. If managed properly, these path-breaking cooperative arrangements could also serve to challenge city governments and local banking systems to increase their investments and services in these underserved communities, thereby dramatically improving the condition of the community.

While there are noted examples of single churches pooling their congregation's resources to improve conditions in their communities, like the Reverend Floyd Flake's Allen African Methodist Episcopal church in Queens, New York, too often church leaders let petty rivalries, projects with narrow goals, financial ignorance and general distrust get in the way of collaborative relationships with other churches that could uplift entire cities or even regions. So, at the end of the day each church stands alone and the impact of those that attempt to conduct good works in their communities is limited. The irony of this situation is that the collective empowerment approach of the churches could lead to not only significant change in terms of community development, it could also result in tremendous financial returns that could enhance the revenue of the churches even while they are maximizing their activities in the community. Civic, fraternal, professional and community organizations can also pursue the idea of maximizing resources through collective action as a way to strengthen their organizations and communities.

In order to reach a point where a community can plan strategies for success that maximize networking opportunities, its members must first define the nature of the problem(s) that they share in common. For many populations, the common problem may be poverty, hunger, failing schools, unsafe neighborhoods, inadequate housing, drugs, preventable chronic illnesses, or all of the above. Once these problems are defined, community members must develop a common agenda that lists the problems and proposed solutions for them. For cities across the U.S., the agenda may include anti-poverty, affordable housing, community development, and community health programs, among many other proposals. Whatever the goal or set of objectives, therefore, members of a community experience a set of common circumstances that give them a vested interest in defining an agenda that can address their predicament.

After problems are defined and an agenda is shaped, members of a community must also realize that they need each other to move the agenda forward. As has been previously stated, the efforts of a single individual or a few individuals may be needed to build momentum, but it will not be enough to carry the agenda to the finish line. Since everyone has a stake in the success of the agenda, from elected officials, citizens and businesses to social activists and associations, a community will need to build upon the core strengths of its members in order to further the cause and make a positive difference.

Developing a comprehensive political strategy for achieving and maintaining the agenda is the next step in the empowerment process. This political action plan first involves identifying individuals, organizations, and institutions that will be important for moving the agenda forward. Based on that assessment, a lobbying/advocacy plan should be established that outlines the pressure points that will yield the greatest returns in terms of creating support for the established agenda. What follows is an execution or action strategy that employs all disposable resources to maximize political effectiveness. Finally, an often forgotten but extremely important part of a political action strategy involves conducting regular maintenance on the plan so that the agenda can be strengthened and possibly institutionalized over time.

Unfortunately, we have seen too many examples of groups working hard to achieve political and policy goals only to see their achievements washed away by a misguided belief that they can relax once the goal has been accomplished. In order to avoid this fate, the Hip Hop Generation must view political action strategies as a deliberate and sustained strategic planning process that may require a long-term, multi-racial, multi-ethnic or even perhaps multi-generational investment in time, energy and money.

It is important to remember that a fundamental requirement of networking and coalition-building is community involvement. It is fine to have grand plans for change, but at the end of the day it is active participation in community events such as Parent Teacher Association (PTA), school board, neighborhood, and city council meetings that will provide the building blocks for successful networking. The people you meet and the skills you build from becoming active in your community will serve you well in your efforts to influence leaders and implement change. Thus, when all is said and done, the H^2G will be most effective in achieving our goals if we include networking as an essential part of the community empowerment equation.

POINTS TO REMEMBER

1. Networking helps individuals and groups to work together to achieve common goals.
2. Coalition building is the ultimate networking strategy for community success.
3. Dedicated individuals who possess a "we" mentality are key to the networking equation.
4. Communities must maximize networking opportunities by:
   a. Defining the problems
   b. Developing a common agenda
   c. Building upon its collective strength to further the cause
   d. Crafting a comprehensive political strategy for achieving and maintaining the agenda
   e. Acting on the outlined strategy
5. Attend and participate in community meetings!

RESOURCES

Internet

Congressional Black Caucus Foundation   www.cbcfinc.org
(Get information about its annual, issue-based networking conference)

Congressional Hispanic Caucus Institute   www.chci.org
(Get information about its annual, issue-based networking conference)

Women's Information Network   www.winonline.org
(Get plugged into a group of politically-minded youthful Washington-DC women)

Books

Fisher, Donna, and Sandy Vilas. <u>Power Networking Second Edition: 59 Secrets for Personal and Professional Success</u>. Bard Press, 2000.

Fraser, George. <u>Success Runs in Our Race: The Complete Guide to Effective Networking in the African American Community</u>. Quill, 1996.

Kimbro, Dennis. <u>What Makes the Great Great: Strategies for Extraordinary Achievement</u>. Main Street Books, 1998.

"Tell me what you gon do to get free, we need more than MC's
We need Hueys, and revolutionaries"
Dead Prez, "We Want Freedom." <u>Let's Get Free</u>. Relativity (2000)

Verse 9: The Organizational Hook Up

While working in the banking industry in his 20's, John Bryant
saw that inner-city neighborhoods in the Los Angeles area lacked
access to banks where residents could open accounts, deposit money,
and make other day-to-day financial transactions. At the same time,
he also saw that many low-income urban residents were not
knowledgeable about fundamental aspects of financial education such
as balancing checkbooks, establishing savings, purchasing homes,
using credit properly and the like. Responding to these perceived
needs, John developed a vision to create a new banking model that
would provide services to underserved communities through a
nonprofit organizational structure. Upon its founding in 1992, John
named his new organization Operation HOPE, Inc.

Twelve years later, Operation HOPE programs have grown to
accommodate the vision of its founder. With more than 50 employees
and over 100 partners, the organization has received millions of dollars
in corporate, government, and individual support and has launched
celebrated programs to promote economic empowerment in
underserved communities across the U.S. One hallmark initiative
called *Banking On Our Future* has taught more than 65,000 young
people financial basics such as how to save money, write checks,
develop budgets, and use credit. Another, called the *Operation HOPE
Banking Centers*, offers residents in low-income Los Angeles
neighborhoods access to one-stop-shopping services that include
checking and savings accounts, check cashing, home loans, and credit
counseling. As a result of his initiative, John Bryant has partnered
with Presidents Bill Clinton and George W. Bush, Federal Reserve
Chairman Alan Greenspan, members of Congress, and many other
leaders from the corporate and nonprofit arenas to promote economic
empowerment in underserved communities.

The Operation HOPE example demonstrates that creating, working
for, or joining an organization can provide an effective way to

81

empower the Hip Hop Generation and bring about positive change. For centuries, groups have formally organized into organizations or associations as a way to pursue common goals that could not be accomplished efficiently by single individuals. In the U.S., organizations as diverse as the Red Cross, the Children's Defense Fund, the YMCA, the Black Panther Party, and Rock the Vote have been created to address unmet needs, problems, issues, and/or to promote a particular philosophy. Despite the many different reasons for which organizations are created, those most active in the U.S. political process can be categorized into three general types: advocacy, direct service or a combination of both.

Information and mobilization are very important in the political world. If you can produce information about your policy preferences and demonstrate that a lot of people support your position, then you can wield a significant amount of power. One of the most efficient ways to reach both of these objectives is through the power of an advocacy organization.

For almost every person, place, or thing that you can imagine, there is an organization that has been created to champion an issue or multiple issues related to the subject. There are advocacy organizations that represent people of color, the elderly, children, guns, the environment, religion, workers, prisoners, corporations, veterans and a multitude of other discrete interests. These organizations can be concerned about a single issue, like affirmative action, or a multitude of issues, such as anti-poverty initiatives, job training programs, and health care access. Whatever the population or issue, these organizations work to develop policy agendas that speak to the needs and interests of their primary constituents and to implement political action strategies that affect policy decisions at the local, state and federal levels.

Advocacy organizations, also called interest groups, play a vital role in the political process for several reasons. First, they serve as a vehicle for mobilizing masses of people in an organized fashion. It is very difficult for an individual working alone to achieve the systemic changes often needed for major policy initiatives. Indeed, it would not be practical for a solo actor to have so much influence that they could implement changes that effect the lives of many others who did not have a say in the matter. In contrast, organizations provide a way to form a consensus among many people, which increases their legitimacy when they assert that "the people" want a policy change. In addition, the resources of an organized membership can be combined to create national, state, and/or local offices with staff that coordinate the activities of the body in a way that promotes achievement of the organization's goals.

Second, advocacy organizations serve as an effective conduit for the creation and dissemination of information. The information flow often works in a multidirectional fashion. Individual members can share information with their local, state, or national offices. These offices can then condense the information from the field into a policy position with supporting research that can then be shared with elected officials and other opinion leaders. Central offices can also be used to gather and distribute information that is of interest to the organization's membership. For example, organization staff can stay abreast of new policy developments and share that information with their membership along with an analysis of how the changes could affect them.

If organization members discover that a policy change has been proposed or enacted that is contrary to their interests, they can then invoke strategic pressure tactics—the third important reason why advocacy organizations are so pivotal to the political process. A large constituency of organization members can place very effective pressure on elected officials who are sensitive to the number of letters, phone calls, or visits that they receive on any given issue. Because of the power and resources that organizations possess, many view mobilized membership organizations as one of the best political counterweights to the influence of the wealthy few. This is so because legislators who receive hundreds or thousands of letters, phone calls or visits on the same topic, know that they can risk losing their positions if they ignore the matter. If a legislator docs not respond to the advocacy efforts of organization members, then the organization's leadership can organize its membership into an effective protest lobby (see Verse 3).

Direct service, or community-based, organizations are just as important as advocacy organizations in the empowerment equation. These organizations most often work at the neighborhood level to offer services that address community needs such as childcare, exercise facilities, free meals for the homeless and senior citizens, and tutoring services for school aged children. As a result of their on-the-ground approach, direct service organizations are often the most experienced with and knowledgeable about the scope and depth of problems facing a community.

Community-based organizations are not only important for their services, but also for the training opportunities and public exposure they can provide for their staff. Instead of standing by waiting for the problems to grow, the staff of direct service organizations often become noted activists themselves as a result of their efforts to convince other organizations and city and state elected officials to direct more private and government resources towards improving the lives of the people they serve. Organization staff can build public recognition while learning how to organize events and provide essential services. There are many examples of noted elected officials and other leaders who have launched their public service careers as a result of the work that they did while serving in a community-based organization. People such as Rev. Floyd Flake, Julian Bond, U.S. Rep. Maxine Waters, and U.S. Rep. Danny K. Davis owe their careers to the exposure and training they received while working in a community-based setting. Thus, participation in these organizations is actually an ideal way for the Hip Hop Generation to develop committed and responsible leaders.

A final reason why community-based organizations are important is that the good works that they produce provide an excellent example for the communities they serve. Not only do those who work for the organization receive an opportunity to see how hard work can pay off, they also give the children in the community a chance to see a positive model for community change and people like them who are working to bring it about. These positive examples of good works in action will influence and empower younger people to remain involved in their communities as they grow up.

84

It is important to note that some direct service organizations also double as advocacy organizations. These organizations gather the information from their community-based programs and use the data to develop materials that can be disseminated to elected officials. This well-researched, experience-based material can provide the basis for compelling policy arguments that may convince officials to enact needed changes. The National Urban League is an example of a hybrid community-based, advocacy organization. The League's local affiliates provide vital services to the community in the form of childcare, after school, senior citizen and job training programs. All the while, the National Urban League maintains a Washington, D.C. office that compiles programmatic information from the field and translates it into a national policy agenda that enables the organization to advocate on behalf of the communities served by their more than 100 affiliates in 34 states across the U.S. Led by former New Orleans Mayor Marc Morial, the National Urban League distributes its evidence-based policy agenda to officials on Capitol Hill through policy publications such as the organization's *State of Black America* and during its annual advocacy gathering in Washington, D.C.

While a plethora of advocacy organizations exist to address a host of issues related to any given subject, it is very likely that the H^2G may still find that none of them advocate on behalf of the people, places or things important to them. Or, an organization may exist that addresses the subject matter, but it does not embody a Hip Hop Generation philosophy or perspective. In this case, it is perfectly appropriate to consider creating a new organization. This new organization may take a number of legal forms. However, some of the most popular organizational structures include a not-for-profit 501 (c) 3, which allows donors to take charitable tax deductions, but prevents organizations from engaging in full-scale partisan political activity, or a 501 (c) 4 that disallows charitable deductions, but enables organizations to engage in expanded forms of political activity. The new organization may also be a for-profit entity that performs community empowerment work while earning a return on its investments. Operation HOPE, Inc. is a complex entity that represents a hybrid of not-for-profit and related for-profit enterprises.

Members of the H^{2}G who think they may be interested in joining or working for an established advocacy organization should do their research to determine whether the organization's policy objectives, institutional culture, and recruitment and advocacy tactics are in line with their values and beliefs. If there is agreement on these matters, working for or joining a membership organization can be a highly rewarding and efficient way to become politically empowered.

In the final analysis, the creation and maintenance of formal organizations will be just as important in furthering the goals of the Hip Hop Generation as it was for the generation before them. While there are many reasons why this is the case, it should be clear that institutional longevity provides a very important reason why organizations remain a vital part of the empowerment equation. When individuals join together to form an institution, the power of their ideas then reside in a structure that can outlast the lives or interests of its founders. The staying power of organizations is particularly important when generations tackle difficult policy issues that will take a long time to achieve. To illustrate this point, the founders of the National Association for the Advancement of Colored People and the National Urban League and were intent on achieving social and political equality for African Americans when they were founded in 1909 and 1910 respectively. Most of the founders, however, died before they could see their policy goals enacted into law with the passage of the Civil Rights Act of 1964 and the Voting Rights Act of 1965. Nevertheless, work related to the spirit and substance of the founders ideals continues to this day and the fact that these organizations continue to function is a testament to the power and relevance of their founding missions.

(Re)SOURCES

Internet

Center for Community Change   www.communitychange.org
(Helps underserved communities build effective organizations and better neighborhoods)

Asian Pacific Americans for Progress   www.apaforprogress.org
(Join a grassroots network of Asian Pacific Americans)

Internal Revenue Service   http://www.irs.gov/charities/index.html
(Get tax information on the various types of organizations that can be created)

Japanese American Citizens League   www.jacl.org
(Get information about maintaining human and civil rights for Americans of Japanese ancestry)

NAACP   www.naacp.org
(Learn how you can join one of the oldest civil rights organizations in
the country)

National Council of La Raza   www.nclr.org
(Join one of the largest constituency-based Hispanic organizations in
the U.S.)

National Council of Negro Women   www.ncnw.org
(Learn about one of the nation's oldest advocacy organizations for and
by African American women)

National Organization for Women   www.now.org
(Join one of the largest organizations dedicated to advocating for
women's issues)

National Urban League   www.nul.org
(Learn about the community programs and advocacy agenda supported
by the League—the nation's second oldest civil rights organization)

Leadership Conference on Civil Rights   www.civilrights.org
(Get information on a multitude of faith-based, civil rights, and other
multi-racial and ethnic organizations dedicated to promoting civil
rights)

Books

Johnson, Ollie and Karin Stanford. <u>Black Political Organizations in
the Post-Civil Rights Era</u>. Rutgers University Press. 2002.

Kaye, Judy and Michael Allison. <u>Strategic Planning for Non Profit
Organizations: A Practical Guide and Workbook</u>. John Wiley
& Sons, Inc. 1997.

Riddle, John. <u>Streetwise Managing a NonProfit: How to Write
Winning Grant Proposals, Work With a Board, and Build a
Fundraising Program</u>. Adams Media Corporation. 2002.

Wolf, Thomas. <u>Managing a NonProfit in the 21st Century</u>.
    Simon & Schuster Publishing. 1999.

THE
HIP HOP
REVOLUTION
IS OUT THERE.

Insert aliens of your choice.

90

"They tell us that our words are scary
They're revolutionary
Because we speak the truth"
Ice-T, "Message to the Soldier." <u>Home Invasion</u>. Priority Records (1993)

Verse 10: Express Yourself!

While attending a recent conference of Afro-descendant legislators in Brazil, I met Sebastion Acaranjo, a young man in his early 40's who was the first Afro-Brazilian to become a Senator in the Sao Paulo State Assembly. Over late night drinks at an outdoor pub, the youthful legislator shared his perceptions about his job and Brazil's shifting political climate with regards to the Afro-Brazilian struggle for racial and economic inclusion.

Although approximately 50 percent of Brazil's population, Afro-Brazilians are 65 percent of the nation's poor, less than 5 percent of the elected officials and less than 2 percent of university graduates.[10] While Brazil has a strong black consciousness movement seeking to promote better opportunities for people of African descent, its membership is relatively small and its ability to mobilize the masses limited by the fact that many Afro-Brazilians do not view the inequalities they experience through the lens of race or racism.

Upon asking the senator how he developed a black consciousness, he shared with me that he had not always understood the role race played in Brazilian society. As a younger man he had remained blissfully unaware of racial discrimination in his country. It wasn't until he began listening to the music and lyrics of Bob Marley, however, that his level of consciousness shifted. Through Marley he was introduced to the concept of racism and began to see clearly how it operated in a Brazilian context. An electrician by trade, the Senator's racial awakening moved him to become more socially engaged and eventually led him to run for political office.

The Senator's story represents a clear example of how artistic expression—Marley's musical lyrics—can influence people's perceptions, beliefs and actions by serving as a vehicle for the mass dissemination of social and political commentary. While the Senator had never traveled to Jamaica, never met or heard Marley in person, he was able to discern the social relevance of Marley's recordings and use the knowledge gained to change his life in a way that could shape the policies that affect the lives of many others.

Today musicians maintain a powerful platform through which they can amplify messages that can open minds, alter behaviors, stimulate action and transform the world. Globalization has promoted the mass consumption of U.S. cultural products—with the style and sound of Hip Hop leading the way. From London and Paris to Tokyo and Nairobi, international audiences are hungry for Hip Hop music's edgy lyrics and infectious beats.

Today, more so than ever before, artists have a platform for reaching millions of people—yet few use their capabilities to promote socially conscious lyrics. Hip Hop has done a good job of highlighting social ills like urban poverty, police brutality and the criminal "injustice" system. Rap artists such as KRS One, Chuck D/Public Enemy, Ice-T, Run DMC, Ice Cube and Tupac Shakur have laid important ground by showing that artists can focus on serious subjects while selling records. Despite their path-breaking contributions, many argue that their politically piercing lyrics (and that of artists like Bob Marley, Marvin Gaye, Gil Scott Heron, Simon and Garfunkel, and Curtis Mayfield) have virtually disappeared in an industry largely intent on promoting a "bling-bling" lifestyle of sex, violence, cars, cash, clothes and jewelry.

Yet, the potential to use art as a tool for social and political change remains great. Marvin Gaye's political commentary in *What's Going On* helped shape public perception of the Vietnam War in the 1970's. Quincy Jones and Michael Jackson used the power of song to help raise funds for children starving in Africa in the 1980's by producing *We Are the World*. Country singer Willie Nelson has raised millions of dollars to help farmers through his "Farm Aid" concerts. Other artists have demonstrated their power to exert political power, raise awareness and money for issues like HIV/AIDS, Parkinson's disease and cancer research by using their talents as a vehicle for expressing their views.

Musicians are not the only people who can reach wide audiences using their creative talents. Sculptors, painters, architects and other artists have also been known to make political statements through their creative products. Consider the skyrocketing career of filmmaker Michael Moore who has developed critically acclaimed documentaries such as *Bowling for Columbine* and *Fahrenheit 9/11* that have covered political subjects such as gun control and the Bush Administration's involvement the Iraq War. His thought-provoking documentaries have touched upon public concerns and interests in such a compelling way that he has transformed the documentary film industry into a multi-million dollar marketable enterprise. And, while the abilities of athletes cannot be readily translated into a political or social context, the notoriety that sports stars receive as a result of their skills also gives them a platform to communicate to a global audience.

Perhaps one of the most unique and talented political voices on the scene at the moment is that of cartoonist Aaron McGruder, the creator of the Boondocks comic strip. Launching his nationally syndicated strip at the tender age of 22, McGruder's insightful political and social commentary covers powerful questions and issues that raises the level of political scrutiny and provide readers with new insight into political matters. From the performance of President George W. Bush and National Security Advisor Condoleeza Rice to the NAACP, McGruder leaves no touchy subject untouched in his attempt to share his perspective with the world.

For those who can't lay a phat rhyme, film a documentary, draw a cartoon, or make the winning touchdown, never fear—your opinions can still be heard. The good news is that if you can write and speak, you can transmit your views about a host of subjects ranging from unjustified wars and stolen elections to ill-advised tax cuts and spending reductions on social programs important to your community.

Writing letters to elected officials to complain, question, expound or propose is one of the most important ways that ordinary citizens can effectively monitor and control the behavior of their elected representatives. Politicians pay close attention to the tone and subject of their constituent mail as it gives them a good sense of how voters in their districts feel about their performance and what issues are most important to them. It is the duty of elected officials and their staffs to respond to the many letters that they receive from the people that elect them to office. Their responses should answer the questions or concerns raised in the letter. If you write to your representative and fail to receive a reply, you know that there is something very wrong with the way your elected representative is running his or her office. If this occurs, you can call the office to inquire about the status of your letter, request an appointment to meet with the official, write another letter, tell others in your community about the lack of response, and/or decide not to vote for that official in the next round of elections.

Writing letters to your local newspaper is another effective way to make your views known. These letters to the editor provide an opportunity for community members to widely share their perspectives about policy and political matters including their opinions about the performance of their elected official. Politicians hate to be embarrassed or put in a position where the decisions they make that may be against the best interests of the community that they serve are made public. Because community leaders and voters read letters to the editor, this mode of expression represents a very powerful tool that can be used to shape public debate on various issues as well as help determine the outcome of elections.

Every single individual has the power to shape public discourse, views, and electoral outcomes by sharing their insight and opinions with the general public and the elected officials who serve them. Musical lyrics, letters to newspapers, poetry, and comic strips are just a few of the methods of communication that individuals can use to empower themselves and their communities. With more access than ever before to the mass media, the Hip Hop Generation is poised to use these various tools of political expression for maximum impact.

(Re)SOURCES

Internet

Congress.org by Capitol Advantage   www.congress.org
(Sound off about politics, get helpful organization tools and information about issues)

MTV Choose or Loose   www.mtv.com/chooseorlose
(Tell folks what you think and learn about MTV's civic engagement efforts)

National Black Caucus of State Legislators   www.nbcsl.org
(Learn about this organization's agenda)

National Conference of State Legislators
(Contact Your State Legislators!)
      http://www.ncsl.org/public/leglinks.cfm

U.S. House of Representatives   http://www.house.gov/writerep/
(Contact Your Member of Congress!)

U.S. Senate   www.senate.gov
(Contact Your U.S. Senator!)

The White House   President@whitehouse.gov
(Tell the President of the United States what you think of his performance!) 202-456-1414

'Wake up!...Why listen to somebody else tell you how to do it
When you can do it yourself; it's all in you, do it, do it"
Nas, "Black Zombie." <u>The Lost Tapes</u>. Sony (2002)

Sequel: Beyond Free-Riders and Coasters

If you want to play the U.S. political game, the 10 action steps outlined in the previous Verses provide the blueprint for gaining unprecedented influence and power. Taken alone, each activity represents a powerful tool to influence aspects of the system. Used together and paired with a well-defined policy agenda, these activities lay the groundwork for a strategic plan that can serve as the basis for real community empowerment.

Despite the untapped potential of this approach, some in the Hip Hop Generation express hostility toward The System because they know how it works against certain communities and has been used to oppress various groups throughout history. Instead of engaging The System, therefore, they say that it makes no sense to participate in America's institutions of government when America makes no effort to do right by them. Yet, these same individuals have not given up their U.S. citizenship nor do they plan to move to another country. Unfortunately, this type of argument creates a false sense of satisfaction and is at the same time self-defeating because it leads to inaction. The satisfaction comes from the ability to denounce a government that you disagree with, but the defeat comes from the fact that that government still controls every single aspect of your life while you still reside within its boundaries. If those who complain about The System without engaging it plan on remaining in the U.S., then their refusal to directly engage The System will forever leave them in a powerless and exploited situation. The Hip Hop Generation must realize that The System is not set up to automatically respond to our needs; it must be made to respond through direct engagement.

While the inside-the-system strategies presented in this book represent one way to make government more responsive to the needs of engaged and active communities, they do not discount the long history of individuals and groups that have sought to achieve power, respect, and justice outside of the U.S. political system. For example,

97

from Martin Delaney and Marcus Garvey to Angela Davis and Imari Obadele, prominent African American historical figures have despaired about the level of equality and human rights afforded blacks in the U.S., and have sought ways to live outside of the U.S. system. Proposals to create new societies in Africa, Latin America and even carving out some land here in the U.S. to establish a nation-state for and by descendants of American slaves have been put forth by intellectual-activists frustrated with the horror of racism in the U.S. Given the historical condition of people of African descent brought to America, it is not surprising that this separatist intellectual tradition has remained alive and well throughout American history. The activities and beliefs of these visionaries must be respected in light of their humanitarian goals.

Despite this separatist tradition, however, many have concluded that their best bet for empowerment lies in exerting pressure upon the current U.S. political system. These proponents argue that because of the tremendous sacrifices, talents, and labor that African Americans, Hispanic Americans, Asian Americans and other racial and ethnic minorities have contributed in the quest to make the U.S. a giant economic and military super-power, they can lay a claim to this country that rivals or exceeds that put forth by European Americans. Another argument offered is that with dedicated effort, these groups have been able to realize some real gains by working the current system in ways that include the activities outlined in the previous Verses.

Because government is supposed to reflect the highest aspirations and ideals of the citizens who give it legitimacy and authority, various groups in American society have made the commitment to fight for the right to receive the full benefits of U.S. citizenship—particularly the right to vote. With these rights, groups that include African Americans, women and others have been able to participate in ways that have forced the systems of government to include their wants and needs into the fabric of the system.

For example, by winning the right to vote and creating an effective advocacy strategy women have organized to enact anti-discrimination policies in the labor market, push for laws that address violence against women, and policies that give women and their families more time off from work without having to worry about being fired for extended absences involving pregnancies and illnesses. None of these measures would likely have been passed into law had women remained voiceless, powerless and excluded from the U.S. political system.

Free-riders and Coasters: Inaction in Action

Even though we have seen how positive things can occur when action is taken, too often individuals and groups view politics from a "free rider" or "coaster" mentality. In the free rider scenario, individuals are concerned about the issues at hand, but do not make the effort to do something about the situation. They look to and depend on the actions of others who may already be working in the area of concern to carry the issue for an entire community. In short, free riders are content to do nothing because they assume someone else will do the work for them and yet they are happy to reap the benefits when the hard work of others pays off.

Even worse, if no one else is actively addressing the problem free riders are content to assume that someone will come along and do something about the problem at some point in the undefined future. The free rider's willingness to stand by and do nothing when no one else has stepped up to the plate to take action is dangerous. For issues left untended eventually worsen as others with a plan of action and a policy agenda hostile to the free rider's interests actively work to do damage to or marginalize the issue at hand in their quest to raise the profile of and gain resources for their own cause.

The coaster is a close cousin of the free rider. The coaster mentality is in play when individuals or groups work hard to push their issues to the top of the national policy agenda only to slack off, or coast, once they feel they have achieved success. Coasters get comfortable by deluding themselves into thinking that the effects of their achievements will last indefinitely. As a result, they imperil the agenda that they helped to build because they have not put a maintenance plan in place to sustain and build upon the policy once enacted.

If there is one thing that is certain in the U.S. political context, it is that the public agenda and the people and opinions that influence it are constantly shifting. The public policy agenda is a very important and dynamic space primarily because a place on the agenda brings legitimacy, tons of money and other resources that will fund issues or causes whatever they may be. Because of the high stakes, people and groups are constantly working to either regain a position of prominence they have lost or achieve a new position of prominence that will displace those at the top. In a race for scarce resources (time, money, energy), only a few issues or groups can dominate space at the top of the public agenda at any given moment. As a result, groups who wish for their issues to retain prominence on the public agenda must work hard to establish institutional mechanisms that will provide continuous support for their issues.

Because hard work and consistent effort is necessary, free riders and coasters are extremely dangerous as they undermine the well being of entire communities by giving up space on the public agenda through sheer lack of effort and planning. As a result, gains that may have been achieved are rolled back and gains that could have been achieved are never fully realized. Evidence of policy roll-backs can be seen in recent threats to the Civil Rights and Women's Rights agendas. Attacks on affirmative action, a woman's right to choose, and attempts to appoint judges that are hostile to these and other important issues represent clear examples of this roll back effort. Evidence of unrealized policy gains can be seen in failing schools, poor health statistics, poverty figures, and in deprived neighborhoods.

At the end of the day, political action is a near zero-sum game—meaning that the stakes can result in a lot or very little if nothing at all. The difference between the two extremes is the amount of collective effort that any one group puts into shaping the public agenda. Success, or receiving a lot, means that the group or groups in question must maintain a constant offense that is consistently working to ensure that appropriate resources and attention are directed towards building strategies that can sustain and build upon the policy agenda. These strategies should also include an effective defense for the times when others seek to threaten the prominence of the agenda at hand.

100

Thus, there is little room for free riders and no room for coasters in this equation if a true community empowerment agenda is to be achieved through political action.

Consequences of Inaction: An Example

The Hip Hop Generation must be especially careful not to fall victim to the free rider or coaster mentalities. Yet, time and again we see evidence of these mentalities in the weak voter turnout from the 40 and under crowd. While individuals certainly have the right to choose not to exercise their voting privileges, it's important that they do so with full knowledge of the consequences.

For this example I reluctantly return to the subject of the students from Prairie View A&M University. As a 1993 graduate of Prairie View A&M University, I was very proud of the 5,000 students who participated in the January 2004 march to protest Waller County District Attorney Oliver Kitzman's illegal stance which maintained that students attending P.V. were not allowed to vote because they were not residents of the county. I was also very embarrassed when the students failed to follow through on their march by taking their protest power to the ballot box during the Waller County primaries a little over a month later. Indeed, news accounts reported that out of about 4,000 registered Prairie View voters, only 10 percent turned out to vote in the March 9, 2004 primaries (preliminary elections that determine the candidates who will run in the general election).[11] Even though these elections were held during spring break, students had an opportunity to participate in early voting conducted on the campus.[12] Yet, by failing to vote early or in the actual primaries registered Prairie View student voters missed an opportunity that could have affirmed their demand for equal voting rights as well as afforded them a chance to vote for those who truly represent their interests.

In short, even though the D.A. settled the lawsuit with paltry concessions to the agitated student population, Prairie View students lost critical ground by coasting on the success of their protest activities and failing to bring the power of those activities to the electoral arena.

Doom and Gloom

The story of my family is irreversibly tied to the history of America. From slavery and Jim Crow to both World Wars and Vietnam. Who I am reflects what America is, has been, and (hopefully) where it is going.

Paducah is the small, dusty West Texas town where much of my family's contemporary history resides. A small, dusty agricultural town, Paducah was once a place where cotton was king and families from miles around the panhandle would come to find economic opportunity either in the cotton fields or in business enterprises created by the cotton boom.

I grew up in a household where my parents took care to share what it was like growing up in Paducah surrounded by the politics and policies of the rural Jim Crow South. My siblings and I listened carefully as they told us stories about how they were made to watch movies from the "Negroes Only" balcony of segregated movie theaters (the best seats in the house they still claim), how they had to leave the movie theater mid-movie to use the nearest "Negroes Only" restroom and water fountain across the street in the basement of the Court House, how they were required to enter stores and restaurants through the "Negroes Only" entrances most often located in the rear of the buildings, and how their families had to carefully plan cross-country trips as their ability to stop for gas, food, or shelter was limited to the very few vendors who would serve "Negroes" on America's interstate highways.

Paducah was also the staging ground for world events that had nothing and everything to do with my family. It was from that town that my mother's oldest brothers and my father's father were called to serve in segregated units during World War II and the Korean War. And it was in Paducah that my father, my uncles, and other male cousins received their draft notices to serve in the armed forces during the Vietnam War.

Paducah is now in an economic freefall, the fortunes of its modest population reversed by technological advances in the cotton industry, the urbanization of America and falling international demand for pricey American cotton. To drive through its downtown today, one is struck by the number of formerly-thriving businesses that have ceased to exist. Paducah's economy is now kept on life support by a county courthouse, senior citizen's home, gas station, grocery store, an elementary/high school, and the few cotton farmers who continue to till their fields on the outskirts of town.

I tell the story of this rural West Texas town because the development of my personal political consciousness is tied as much to the condition of its people as it is to the history of blacks in America. According to the 2000 Census, 32 percent of Paducah's population is Black or Hispanic, approximately 61 percent have only a high school degree, unemployment hovers around 7 percent (at least two times higher for African Americans and Hispanics), and the median household income is a mere $23,000. As jobs disappeared over the years, opportunities—particularly for low-skilled workers—became scarce and those who remain often rely on government social insurance and safety net programs like Social Security, Supplemental Security Insurance (SSI), Food Stamps, and Temporary Assistance for Needy Families (TANF) to help make ends meet.

There are communities in cities across America whose residents face similar obstacles to social and economic advancement. Members of these urban communities—most often African Americans and Hispanics—also lack economic opportunity in the face of poverty exacerbated by high unemployment rates, failing schools, inability to access quality healthcare and the loss of viable jobs to technological advances, corporate downsizing and/or overseas competition. Individuals in these communities are often left scrambling to survive under bleak circumstances caused by political and business decisions made at the macro level.

It is a fact that the Hip Hop Generation living in underserved urban and rural communities today are being poorly prepared for life in a new century. As a result, a vast majority of these young people are not and will not be prepared to successfully compete for the high skilled jobs in the new twenty-first century economy. Their socioeconomic circumstances will be further eroded by their inability to access job-related perks such as retirement benefits, disability benefits, health insurance, and other tax-preferred savings vehicles. And, barring

103

implementation of a policy that would export U.S. workers to countries in the world where unskilled labor is still marketable, these populations will have fewer choices in a future that may have even less public resources available for government assistance programs. Thus, uneducated, unhealthy and unemployed with little public assistance, the only opportunities available for those left behind will likely lie in an underground economy that inevitably leads to further social and economic exclusion and possibly the isolation of prison.

A Hip Hop Policy Agenda

Much of this book has been focused on the action steps that the Hip Hop Generation needs to take to launch an effective political action strategy. Political action, however, must be accompanied by a policy agenda that addresses outstanding needs and goals if the H^{2}G wants to avoid a doomsday future where we are irrelevant and isolated. It is important, therefore, to outline a policy agenda that speaks to the needs of the Hip Hop Generation.

Before one can outline a policy agenda, it is imperative to envision the type of community and society in which the Hip Hop Generation wants to live. Unfortunately, too many have become accustomed to looking backward or focusing on the present without seeing how things can be changed for the future. Members of the H^{2}G should ask themselves: If society could be the way that I envision it what would it look like? What kind of future would I want for my children? Would I want them to have a world that is better than the world that exists for me? This vision quest exercise is an essential pre-condition for establishing a policy agenda, as it would be highly ineffective to develop the agenda without having a vision or goal for the future that the agenda is supposed to help bring about.

Many groups and organizations with established agendas usually have an underlying philosophy that informs their vision for society. For example, capitalists believe that free markets should regulate most aspects of society and that the role of government should be limited while socialists believe that government should provide many of the services currently regulated by the free market that are important for the common good. The H^{2}G should consider if these or other

104

philosophical approaches most appropriately reflect the types of initiatives that must be undertaken to address the problems that we face.

Once a common vision or philosophy for the future is established, there are several elements that a Hip Hop policy agenda must encompass in order to be effective. First, the agenda must "keep it real" by focusing on the problems young people see in their communities everyday. Second, the agenda must identify the institutional, social, political, and economic factors that feed into the problem. Third, the agenda must develop policy-oriented solutions to the problems while also paying attention to community-oriented solutions. Fourth, the agenda must be connected to a political action strategy that can move the ball down the court toward positive change.

The Hip Hop Generation knows that current policies fall painfully short when it comes to the scope and depth of the problems facing our communities. As a result, there is no shortage of issues that can be addressed through a H^2G policy agenda. Consider the range of issues of concern to the Hip Hop Generation:

HEALTH
Access to Health Care
HIV/AIDS Prevention and Treatment
Eliminating Health Disparities (e.g. Type II diabetes, heart disease, stroke)
Drug Prevention and Treatment
Violence Prevention and Anger Management
EDUCATION
Promoting Educational Achievement
Quality Educational Facilities
Quality School Teachers
Access to Multi-Cultural and Bi-Lingual Education
Special Education Tracking Policies
Access to Higher Education
COMMUNITY (IN) JUSTICE
Crack-Cocaine Sentencing Disparities
Racial Profiling

Excessive Law Enforcement Tactics
Reforming the Prison Industrial Complex
ECONOMIC DEVELOPMENT
Wealth Creation
Homeownership and Affordable Housing
Predatory Lending
Entrepreneurship
Credit Awareness/Financial Literacy
Job Training
SOCIAL EQUITY
Felon Disenfranchisement
Voter Protection
Affirmative Action
Discriminatory Immigration Policy
Improving the Social Safety Net (e.g. Social Security, SSI, TANF, Section 8 and Food Stamp Programs)

Given the many problems that exist, the first step in building a policy agenda is to list the problems that can be addressed through the political arena. Problems such as incarceration, drug use, and violence in the schools are cornerstone policy issues that must be included. Yet, there are also a number of government programs that intersect with these problems in ways that impact the lives of young people and their families that must also be examined to determine how they help or harm community wellbeing and whether they should be reformed, rebuilt or eliminated.

In line with enumerating the problems to be addressed is examining problems closely to understand how social, political, economic, and other structural factors play into each situation. It is impossible to arrive at an effective solution without understanding the multitude of factors that may contribute to the problem. Understanding contributing factors also helps determine whether the solution should be policy-oriented, community-oriented or both. For example, a policy-oriented solution that seeks to increase access to college may focus on expanding the Pell Grant program while a community-oriented solution to the same issue may create a high school tutoring program that prepares students for the Scholastic Achievement Test (SAT) or a program that seeks to change student's negative attitudes towards educational achievement. Depending on how it's structured, the policy-oriented solution could also include the community-based solutions by issuing government grants that promote programs supporting young people's access to colleges and universities.

Finally, a H^2G policy agenda would have to be linked to a well-thought-out political strategy in order for it to get anywhere. So, the elements laid out in the previous 10 Verses of this book would have to be implemented in a way that effectively layers the policy agenda on top of an integrated voting, fundraising, lobbying/advocacy, networking and communication strategy that moves the Hip Hop Generation towards our vision for the future.

Conclusion

In a previous publication examining the effectiveness of the Congressional Black Caucus (CBC) in furthering a post-Civil Rights agenda that includes HIV/AIDS, I wrote:

"It would seem, as Civil Rights leaders [evidently] believed, that simple inclusion would have ensured that the needs of African Americans would be incorporated systemically and taken care of through the normal democratic process. The fact that the CBC frequently employs protest tactics (i.e. actions outside the context of normal Congressional civility/norms) in order to achieve even modest gains demonstrates that the system operates on a pattern of values and norms that do not normally include black concerns. This situation indicates that the demands presented by the CBC are not within the mainstream of the overall decision-making process. An explanation for this dilemma may lie in what can be termed "institutional conditioning." This process means that after the rise of a social movement resulting in substantive gains for the contesting group, the system must become accustomed to processing the new values, demands, and expectations posed by the newly incorporated group. This newly incorporated group, however, cannot realize benefits until

*it is effective in targeting all of the pressure points needed to ensure
reflexive institutional responsiveness. In other words, the system must
receive pressure at all of the points where it is accustomed to meeting
group demands and needs. When this pressure is applied, the system
should be able to handle these demands seamlessly and at times even
anticipate them. This is this state of democracy that Civil Rights
leaders envisioned."[13]*

I went on to say that African Americans, nor many other
historically marginalized groups, have yet to reach this vision of
democracy primarily because the Civil Rights Movement did not result
in efforts to implement a multi-pronged strategy for placing pressure
on The System. The Hip Hop Generation must correct this fatal
tactical error.

Voting, grassroots protest, candidate recruitment and development,
issue lobbying, fundraisers and political action committees,
community networking, institution building, and civic communication
are all factors that could bring additional pressures on The System. It
is the responsibility of the Hip Hop Generation to fully develop these
factors in order to achieve a state of true democracy where the systems
of government are conditioned to reflexively meet the needs of all
communities.

The Hip Hop Generation has a stark choice: It can either fall on
the sword of materialism and narcissism that currently occupies much
of its attention and risk a future where members will be slaves to
poverty, ignorance, and disease. Or, it can adopt a philosophy of
community activism and collective well being that seeks to build
wealth, health and opportunity for the Hip Hop Generation and for
generations to come. Conscious minds would say that this is no choice
at all.

The H^{2}G must come to realize that the life imagined in even the
fanciest videos will not hold a candle to the quantum possibilities that
can be realized through strategic and sustained political activism. Yet
the Hip Hop Generation must still get to a point where activism
becomes second nature—a compulsive habit, like putting on clothes
every morning—that becomes ingrained in its collective psyche. We

must not only embrace this philosophy for ourselves, we must also be responsible for teaching our children the importance of civic engagement so that the political baton can be passed to future generations without losing precious time or sacrificing the agenda. Thus, members of the H^{2}G must take our children with us to the polls and community events, let them listen to and participate in political discussions, and encourage them to read extensively so that they too will be prepared to engage in the political process.

When it comes to our families, our neighborhoods, and our jobs, the Hip Hop Generation should demand the best and expect nothing less. As it stands today, many of us live a second-class life where we have come to accept and even expect a cut-rate existence. There is absolutely no reason why this state of internalized oppression has to continue. The Hip Hop Generation must realize that America belongs to us just as much as it belongs to any other group. With ownership, however, comes the responsibility of leadership. It is time for the Hip Hop Generation to assume its position at the helm of America to steer it into a better future where everyone is treated equally and where all children can reach their fullest potential. This can only be accomplished through full-throttle political action.

REFERENCES

[1] Kitwana, Bakari. <u>The Hip Hop Generation: Young Blacks and the Crisis in African American Culture</u>. New York: Basic Books, 2002.

[2] U.S. Census Bureau. "Voting and Registration in the Election of November 2000," February, 2002.

[3] Ibid.

[4] Study conducted by Washington Post, Henry J. Kaiser Family Foundation and Harvard University, 2002.

[5] Stewart, Sherrel W. "Prairie View Students to March for Voting Rights," BlackAmericaWeb.com, January 2004. (http://www.blackamericaweb.com/site.aspx/bawnews/pvvoting)

[6] http://www.constitutioncenter.org/constitution/ This Interactive Constitution is based on *The Words We Live By: Your Annotated Guide to the Constitution* by Linda R. Monk (Hyperion/A Stonesong Press Book). Copyright © 2003 Linda R. Monk and The Stonesong Press, Inc.

[7] Ibid.

[8] Ibid.

[9] Hope Franklin, John and Genna Rae McNeil, eds. <u>African Americans and the Living Constitution</u>. Washington, DC: Smithsonian Institution Press, 1995.

[10] Global Rights. "Brazil Takes Next Steps Toward Equal Opportunity for All," Affirmative Action in the Americas, April 2004. (www.globalrights.org)

[11] Stewart, Sherrel W. "Black Young People Registering But Not Voting," BlackAmericaWeb.com, March 9, 2004. (http://www.blackamericaweb.com/site.aspx/bawnews/pvstory)

[12] Crowe, Robert, "Students Seek Three Days of Early Voting Near Prairie View Campus," Houston Chronicle, February 12, 2004.

[13] Rockeymoore, Maya. <u>The African American Political Response to HIV and AIDS: A Study of the Congressional Black Caucus in the 105th Congress</u>. Dissertation, Purdue University, 2000.

INDEX